Baking

Publications International, Ltd.

Louis Weber, CEO
Publications International, Ltd.
8140 Lehigh Ave
Morton Grove, IL 60053

Pictured on the front cover: Lemon Pound Cake *(page 58).*

Pictured on the back cover *(clockwise from left):* Super Chocolate Cookies *(page 24),* Blueberry Muffins *(page 132),* Red Velvet Brownies *(page 40)* and Olive Herb Pull-Aparts *(page 176).*

ISBN: 978-1-63938-997-1

Manufactured in China.

8 7 6 5 4 3 2 1

Microwave Cooking: Microwave ovens vary in wattage. Use the cooking times as guidelines and check for doneness before adding more time.

WARNING: Food preparation, baking and cooking involve inherent dangers: misuse of electric products, sharp electric tools, boiling water, hot stoves, allergic reactions, foodborne illnesses and the like, pose numerous potential risks. Publications International, Ltd. (PIL) assumes no responsibility or liability for any damages you may experience as a result of following recipes, instructions, tips or advice in this publication.

While we hope this publication helps you find new ways to eat delicious foods, you may not always achieve the results desired due to variations in ingredients, cooking temperatures, typos, errors, omissions or individual cooking abilities.

Let's get social!

@Publications_International

@PublicationsInternational

www.pilbooks.com

Contents

Cookies

Old-Fashioned Oatmeal Cookies

makes 3 dozen cookies

2 cups old-fashioned oats
1⅓ cups all-purpose flour
¾ teaspoon baking soda
½ teaspoon baking powder
½ teaspoon salt
1 cup packed brown sugar
¾ cup (1½ sticks) butter, softened
¼ cup granulated sugar
1 egg
1 tablespoon honey
1 teaspoon vanilla

1 Preheat oven to 350°F. Line cookie sheets with parchment paper. Whisk oats, flour, baking soda, baking powder and salt in medium bowl.

2 Beat brown sugar, butter and granulated sugar in large bowl with electric mixer at medium speed until light and fluffy. Add egg, honey and vanilla; beat until well blended. Gradually add flour mixture at low speed, beating just until blended. Drop dough by tablespoonfuls about 2 inches apart on prepared cookie sheets.

3 Bake 11 to 15 minutes or until cookies are puffed and golden. Cool on cookie sheets 5 minutes. Remove to wire racks; cool completely.

Red Velvet Cookies

makes about 15 cookies

- 1¼ cups plus 2 tablespoons all-purpose flour
- 2 tablespoons unsweetened cocoa powder
- ½ teaspoon baking soda
- ½ teaspoon salt
- ¼ teaspoon instant coffee granules or espresso powder
- ½ cup (1 stick) butter, melted
- ½ cup packed brown sugar
- ¼ cup granulated sugar
- 1 egg
- 1 teaspoon vanilla
- 1½ teaspoons red food coloring gel *or* 2 teaspoons liquid red food coloring
- 1 teaspoon white vinegar
- 1 cup white chocolate chips, divided

1 Preheat oven to 350°F. Line two cookie sheets with parchment paper. Whisk flour, cocoa, baking soda, salt and coffee granules in medium bowl.

2 Whisk butter, brown sugar and granulated sugar in large bowl until well blended and smooth. Whisk in egg and vanilla until blended. Add food coloring and vinegar; whisk until well blended. Add flour mixture; stir until blended. Stir in ¾ cup white chips.

3 Using scant 3 tablespoons dough per cookie, scoop dough into balls* (slightly larger than a golf ball; balls should not be smooth). Place 2 inches apart on prepared cookie sheets; press additional white chips into top of each cookie.

4 Bake 8 minutes or until cookies are slightly puffy in center. Lift cookie sheets up several inches and let them drop down on oven racks, deflating centers of cookies. Bake 3 to 5 minutes or until edges of cookies are set. Lift and drop cookie sheets again on countertop before removing to wire racks. Cool completely on cookie sheets.

**Use plastic gloves while working with dough to avoid staining your hands.*

Chocolate Caramel Thumbprint Cookies

makes 2½ dozen cookies

Cookies

1½ cups all-purpose flour
¾ cup unsweetened cocoa powder
½ teaspoon salt
1 cup (2 sticks) butter, softened
⅔ cup packed brown sugar
2 eggs, separated
1 teaspoon vanilla
2 cups finely chopped pecans

Caramel Filling

½ cup packed brown sugar
¼ cup (½ stick) butter
2 tablespoons whipping cream
Pinch of salt
2 tablespoons powdered sugar

1 Preheat oven to 375°F. Line cookie sheets with parchment paper or leave ungreased. Whisk flour, cocoa and ½ teaspoon salt in medium bowl.

2 Beat 1 cup butter and ⅔ cup brown sugar in large bowl with electric mixer at medium speed until light and fluffy. Beat in egg yolks and vanilla until well blended. Gradually add flour mixture at low speed, beating just until blended. Shape level tablespoonfuls of dough into balls.

3 Whisk egg whites in small bowl. Place pecans in medium bowl. Dip balls one at a time into egg whites, turning to coat completely and letting excess drip back into bowl. Roll in pecans to coat. Place on prepared cookie sheets. Press thumb firmly into center of each cookie.

4 Bake about 10 minutes until cookies are set. Quickly repress thumbprints with end of wooden spoon. Cool on cookie sheets 5 minutes. Remove to wire racks; cool completely.

5 For filling, combine ½ cup brown sugar and ¼ cup butter in small saucepan. Cook over medium heat until mixture begins to boil, stirring constantly; boil 1 minute, stirring constantly. Remove from heat. Stir in cream and pinch of salt; cool 15 minutes. Whisk in powdered sugar until smooth. Fill each cookie with about ½ teaspoon filling; let stand until firm.

Danish Raspberry Ribbons

makes about 6 dozen cookies

Cookies

- **1 cup (2 sticks) butter, softened**
- **½ cup granulated sugar**
- **1 egg**
- **2 tablespoons milk**
- **2 teaspoons vanilla**
- **¼ teaspoon almond extract**
- **¼ teaspoon salt**
- **2⅔ cups all-purpose flour**
- **6 tablespoons seedless raspberry jam**

Glaze

- **½ cup powdered sugar**
- **1 tablespoon milk**
- **1 teaspoon vanilla**

1 Beat butter and granulated sugar in large bowl with electric mixer at medium speed until light and fluffy. Beat in egg, 2 tablespoons milk, 2 teaspoons vanilla, almond extract and salt until well blended. Gradually add 1½ cups flour at low speed, beating just until blended. Stir in enough remaining flour with spoon to form stiff dough. Shape dough into disc. Wrap in plastic wrap; refrigerate until firm, at least 30 minutes or overnight.

2 Preheat oven to 375°F. Divide dough into six equal pieces. With floured hands, shape one piece at a time into ¾-inch-thick rope, about 12 inches long. (Keep remaining dough pieces wrapped in refrigerator.) Place ropes 2 inches apart on ungreased cookie sheets. Make ¼-inch-deep groove down center of each rope with handle of wooden spoon or finger.

3 Bake 12 minutes; ropes will flatten to ½-inch-thick strips. Remove from oven; spoon 1 tablespoon jam into each groove. Bake 5 to 7 minutes or until strips are light golden brown. Cool on cookie sheet 15 minutes.

4 For glaze, combine powdered sugar, 1 tablespoon milk and 1 teaspoon vanilla in small bowl; stir until smooth. Drizzle over cookie strips. Let stand 5 minutes or until set. Cut cookie strips at 45-degree angle into 1-inch slices. Place cookies on wire racks; let stand until set.

Cocoa Crinkle Sandwich Cookies

makes about 20 sandwich cookies

Cookies

- 1¾ cups all-purpose flour
- ½ cup unsweetened cocoa powder
- 1 teaspoon baking soda
- ½ teaspoon salt
- ½ cup (1 stick) butter
- 1½ cups granulated sugar, divided
- 2 eggs
- 2 teaspoons vanilla

Frosting

- 2½ cups powdered sugar
- 1 cup (2 sticks) butter, softened
- 2 tablespoons unsweetened cocoa powder
- ½ cup dark chocolate chips, melted and cooled
- 3 tablespoons whipping cream
- 1 teaspoon vanilla
- ⅛ teaspoon salt

1 Whisk flour, ½ cup cocoa, baking soda and ½ teaspoon salt in small bowl.

2 Melt ½ cup butter in large saucepan over medium heat; cool slightly. Add 1¼ cups granulated sugar; whisk until smooth. Add eggs, one at a time, whisking until blended after each addition. Stir in 2 teaspoons vanilla until smooth. Stir in flour mixture just until blended. Cover bowl with plastic wrap; refrigerate 2 hours.

3 Preheat oven to 350°F. Line cookie sheets with parchment paper. Place remaining ¼ cup granulated sugar in shallow bowl. Shape dough into 1-inch balls; roll in sugar. Place 1½ inches apart on prepared cookie sheets.

4 Bake 12 minutes or until set. Cool on cookie sheets 5 minutes. Remove to wire racks; cool completely.

5 For frosting, beat powdered sugar, 1 cup butter and 2 tablespoons cocoa in large bowl with electric mixer at low speed until blended. Add chocolate, cream, 1 teaspoon vanilla and ⅛ teaspoon salt; beat until blended. Increase speed to medium-high; beat about 5 minutes or until light and fluffy.

6 Pipe or spread about 2 tablespoons frosting on flat sides of half of cookies; top with remaining cookies. Store in airtight container in refrigerator.

Chocolate Coconut Almond Macaroons

makes 1½ dozen cookies

1⅓ cups flaked sweetened coconut
⅔ cup sugar
2 egg whites
½ teaspoon vanilla
¼ teaspoon almond extract
¼ teaspoon salt
4 ounces sliced almonds, coarsely chopped
18 whole almonds
½ cup semisweet chocolate chips
¼ cup whipping cream

1 Combine coconut, sugar, egg whites, vanilla, almond extract and salt in medium bowl; mix well. Fold in sliced almonds. Cover and refrigerate at least 1 hour or overnight.

2 Preheat oven to 350°F. Line cookie sheet with parchment paper.

3 Shape tablespoonfuls of dough into balls. Place 1 inch apart on prepared cookie sheet. Press 1 whole almond on top of each cookie.

4 Bake 15 minutes or until lightly browned. Cool on cookie sheet 5 minutes. Remove to wire rack; cool completely.

5 Meanwhile for ganache, place chocolate chips in shallow bowl. Heat cream in small saucepan until bubbles form around edge. Pour cream over chocolate; let stand 2 minutes. Stir until smooth. Let cool 10 to 15 minutes.

6 Dip bottom of each cookie into ganache. Place cookies onto clean parchment- or waxed paper-lined cookie sheet. Refrigerate until ganache is set. Store in airtight container in refrigerator.

Black and White Sandwich Cookies

makes about 2 dozen sandwich cookies

Cookies

1¼ cups (2½ sticks) butter
¾ cup superfine or granulated sugar
1 egg
1½ teaspoons vanilla
¼ teaspoon salt
2⅓ cups all-purpose flour, divided
⅓ cup unsweetened cocoa powder

Filling

½ cup (1 stick) butter
4 ounces cream cheese, softened
2 cups plus 2 tablespoons powdered sugar
2 tablespoons unsweetened cocoa powder

1 For cookies, beat 1¼ cups butter and superfine sugar in large bowl with electric mixer until creamy. Beat in egg, vanilla and salt until well blended. Gradually add 2 cups flour at low speed, beating just until blended.

2 Remove half of dough to medium bowl; stir in remaining ⅓ cup flour. Add ⅓ cup cocoa to dough in mixer bowl; beat just until blended. Wrap doughs separately in plastic wrap; refrigerate 30 minutes or until firm.

3 Preheat oven to 350°F. Roll out plain dough on floured surface to ¼-inch thickness. Cut out 1- to 2-inch circles; place 2 inches apart on nonstick cookie sheet. Repeat with chocolate dough.

4 Bake 8 to 10 minutes or until set but not browned. Immediately remove to wire racks; cool completely.

5 For filling, beat ½ cup butter and cream cheese in medium bowl with electric mixer until well blended. Add 2 cups powdered sugar; beat until creamy. Remove half of filling to small bowl; stir in remaining 2 tablespoons powdered sugar. Add 2 tablespoons cocoa to filling in mixer bowl; beat until smooth.

6 Pipe or spread chocolate frosting on flat side of half of plain cookies; top with remaining plain cookies. Pipe or spread vanilla frosting on flat side of half of chocolate cookies; top with remaining chocolate cookies. Store in airtight container in refrigerator.

Peanutty Chocolate-Orange Sandwich Cookies

makes about 4 dozen sandwich cookies

Cookies

3 cups all-purpose flour
2 teaspoons baking soda
½ teaspoon salt
4 ounces cream cheese, softened
1 cup (2 sticks) butter, softened
1 cup packed dark brown sugar
¾ cup granulated sugar
2 eggs
1 teaspoon vanilla
1 cup peanut butter
2½ cups whole unsalted peanuts

Orange-Chocolate Filling

4 ounces cream cheese, softened
½ cup (1 stick) butter, softened
1 tablespoon vanilla
Grated peel of 1 orange
1 package (16 ounces) powdered sugar
4 ounces bittersweet chocolate, melted

1 Whisk flour, baking soda and salt in medium bowl.

2 Beat 4 ounces cream cheese and 1 cup butter in large bowl with electric mixer at medium speed until creamy. Add brown sugar and granulated sugar; beat 3 to 5 minutes or until light and fluffy. Add eggs and vanilla; beat until well blended. Beat in 1 cup peanut butter. Gradually add flour mixture at low speed, beating just until blended. Stir in peanuts. Cover and refrigerate 3 hours or overnight.

3 Preheat oven to 350°F. Line cookie sheets with parchment paper. Shape tablespoonfuls of dough into balls. Place 1 inch apart on prepared cookie sheets.

4 Bake 8 to 10 minutes or until set. Cool on cookie sheets 2 minutes. Remove to wire racks; cool completely.

5 For filling, beat 4 ounces cream cheese and ½ cup butter in large bowl with electric mixer at medium speed until smooth. Beat in vanilla and

orange peel at low speed until blended. Gradually add powdered sugar at low speed; beat at high speed about 5 minutes or until very fluffy. Beat in melted chocolate at low speed until blended. Pipe or spread heaping tablespoon filling on flat side of half of cookies; top with remaining cookies.

Chocolate-Coconut-Toffee Delights

makes 1 dozen large cookies

- ½ cup all-purpose flour
- ¼ teaspoon baking powder
- ¼ teaspoon salt
- 1 package (12 ounces) semisweet chocolate chips, divided
- ¼ cup (½ stick) butter, cut into small pieces
- ¾ cup packed brown sugar
- 2 eggs
- 1 teaspoon vanilla
- 1½ cups flaked sweetened coconut
- 1 cup toffee baking bits
- ½ cup bittersweet chocolate chips

1 Preheat oven to 350°F. Line cookie sheets with parchment paper. Whisk flour, baking powder and salt in small bowl.

2 Combine 1 cup semisweet chocolate chips and butter in medium microwavable bowl. Microwave on HIGH 1 minute; stir. Microwave at additional 30-second intervals until mixture is melted and smooth, stirring after each interval.

3 Beat brown sugar, eggs and vanilla in large bowl with electric mixer at medium speed until creamy. Beat in chocolate mixture until well blended. Gradually add flour mixture at low speed, beating just until blended. Stir in coconut, toffee bits and remaining 1 cup semisweet chocolate chips. Drop dough by heaping ⅓ cupfuls 3 inches apart onto prepared cookie sheets. Flatten into 3½-inch circles with spatula.

4 Bake 15 to 17 minutes or until edges are firm. Cool on cookie sheets 2 minutes; slide parchment paper and cookies onto wire racks to cool completely.

5 For chocolate drizzle, place bittersweet chocolate chips in small microwavable bowl. Microwave on HIGH 30 seconds; stir. Microwave at additional 30-second intervals until melted and smooth, stirring after each interval. Drizzle chocolate over cookies with fork. Let stand until set.

Pistachio Lemon Shortbread Cookies

makes 3 dozen cookies

- 1 cup (2 sticks) butter, softened
- ½ cup packed brown sugar
- ¼ cup powdered sugar
- Grated peel of 1 lemon
- ½ teaspoon salt
- ½ teaspoon vanilla
- 2 cups all-purpose flour
- 1¼ cups coarsely chopped pistachios, toasted
- ½ cup white chocolate chips

1 Preheat oven to 300°F. Line cookie sheets with parchment paper or leave ungreased.

2 Beat butter, brown sugar and powdered sugar in large bowl with electric mixer at medium-high speed 5 minutes or until light and fluffy. Add lemon peel, salt and vanilla; mix well. Gradually add flour mixture at low speed, beating just until blended. Stir in pistachios and white chips.

3 Shape dough by tablespoons into 1-inch balls; place on cookie sheets and flatten slightly with fingers.

4 Bake 15 minutes or until lightly browned around edges. Cool on cookie sheets 5 minutes. Remove to wire racks; cool completely.

Super Chocolate Cookies

makes about 20 cookies

- 2 cups all-purpose flour
- ⅓ cup unsweetened cocoa powder
- 1 teaspoon baking soda
- ½ teaspoon salt
- 1⅓ cups packed brown sugar
- 1 cup (2 sticks) butter, softened
- 2 eggs
- 2 teaspoons vanilla
- 1 cup candy-coated chocolate pieces
- 1 cup dried cranberries, dried cherries and/or raisins
- ¾ cup salted peanuts, chopped

1 Preheat oven to 350°F. Whisk flour, cocoa, baking soda and salt in medium bowl.

2 Beat brown sugar and butter in large bowl with electric mixer at medium speed until light and fluffy. Add eggs and vanilla; beat until well blended. Gradually add flour mixture, beating at low speed just until blended. Stir in chocolate pieces, cranberries and peanuts.

3 Drop dough by ¼ cupfuls 3 inches apart onto ungreased cookie sheets. Flatten slightly with fingertips.

4 Bake 13 to 15 minutes or until almost set. Cool on cookie sheets 2 minutes. Remove to wire racks; cool completely.

Rosemary Honey Shortbread Cookies

makes 2 dozen cookies

2 cups all-purpose flour

1 tablespoon fresh rosemary leaves,* minced

½ teaspoon salt

½ teaspoon baking powder

¾ cup (1½ sticks) butter, softened

½ cup powdered sugar

2 tablespoons honey

***For best flavor, use only fresh rosemary or substitute fresh or dried lavender buds.**

1 Whisk flour, rosemary, salt and baking powder in medium bowl.

2 Beat butter, powdered sugar and honey in large bowl with electric mixer at medium speed until creamy. Add flour mixture; beat at low speed just until blended. (Mixture will be crumbly.) Shape dough into a log. Wrap in plastic wrap; refrigerate 1 hour or until firm. (Dough can be refrigerated several days before baking.)

3 Preheat oven to 350°F. Line cookie sheets with parchment paper. Cut dough into ½-inch slices; place 2 inches apart on prepared cookie sheets.

4 Bake 13 minutes or until set. Cool on cookie sheets 1 minute. Remove to wire racks; cool completely.

Brownies & Bars

Seven-Layer Bars

makes 2 to 3 dozen bars

2 cups graham cracker crumbs
½ cup (1 stick) butter, melted
1 teaspoon vanilla
1 cup butterscotch chips
1 cup chocolate chips
1 cup shredded sweetened coconut
1 cup chopped walnuts or pecans
1 can (14 ounces) sweetened condensed milk

1 Preheat oven to 350°F. Line 13×9-inch baking pan with parchment paper or spray with nonstick cooking spray.

2 Combine graham crackers crumbs, butter and vanilla in medium bowl; mix well. Press mixture evenly onto bottom of prepared pan. Top with butterscotch chips, chocolate chips, coconut and nuts. Pour condensed milk evenly over nuts.

3 Bake 25 minutes or until lightly browned. Cool completely in pan on wire rack. Remove from pan using parchment; cut into bars.

Key Lime Bars

makes 2 to 3 dozen bars

- 1½ cups finely crushed graham crackers (10 to 12 crackers)
- ¼ cup packed brown sugar
- 2 tablespoons all-purpose flour
- 5 tablespoons melted butter
- 1 package (8 ounces) cream cheese, softened
- 1½ cups granulated sugar
- 2 eggs
- ¼ cup Key lime juice
- 1 tablespoon grated lime peel
- Lime slices (optional)

1 Preheat oven to 350°F. Spray 13×9-inch baking pan with nonstick cooking spray.

2 For crust, combine graham cracker crumbs, brown sugar and flour in large bowl. Add melted butter; stir until crackers are moist and crumbly. Press mixture evenly onto bottom of prepared pan. Bake 15 minutes.

3 Meanwhile, beat cream cheese and granulated sugar in bowl with electric mixer at medium-low speed until smooth and creamy. Add eggs, one at a time, beating well after each addition. Add lime juice and lime peel; beat just until blended. Pour filling over warm crust.

4 Bake 15 to 20 minutes or until filling is set and begins to pull away from sides of pan. Cool on wire rack 2 hours. Cut into bars; garnish with lime slices. Store in airtight container in refrigerator.

Caramel Chocolate Chunk Blondies

makes 2 to 3 dozen bars

- **1½ cups all-purpose flour**
- **1 teaspoon baking powder**
- **1 teaspoon salt**
- **¾ cup granulated sugar**
- **¾ cup packed brown sugar**
- **½ cup (1 stick) butter, softened**
- **2 eggs**
- **1½ teaspoons vanilla**
- **1 package (11½ ounces) semisweet chocolate chunks *or* 10 ounces chopped bittersweet chocolate**
- **5 tablespoons caramel ice cream topping**
- **Flaky sea salt (optional)**

1 Preheat oven to 350°F. Line 13×9-inch baking pan with parchment paper or spray with nonstick cooking spray. Whisk flour, baking powder and 1 teaspoon salt in medium bowl.

2 Beat granulated sugar, brown sugar and butter in large bowl with electric mixer at medium speed until smooth and creamy. Beat in eggs and vanilla until well blended. Gradually add flour mixture at low speed, beating just until blended. Stir in chocolate chunks.

3 Spread batter evenly in prepared pan. Drop spoonfuls of caramel topping over batter; swirl into batter with butter knife or small offset spatula. Sprinkle with sea salt, if desired.

4 Bake about 30 minutes or until edges are golden brown (center will be puffed and will not look set). Cool completely in pan on wire rack. Remove from pan using parchment; cut into bars.

Lemon Iced Ambrosia Bars

makes 2 to 3 dozen bars

1¾ cups all-purpose flour, divided
2⅓ cups powdered sugar, divided
½ teaspoon salt, divided
¾ cup (1½ sticks) cold butter
2 cups packed brown sugar
4 eggs
1 cup flaked sweetened coconut
1 cup finely chopped pecans
½ teaspoon baking powder
2 cups powdered sugar
3 tablespoons lemon juice
2 tablespoons butter, softened

1 Preheat oven to 350°F. Spray 13×9-inch baking pan with nonstick cooking spray.

2 Combine 1½ cups flour, ⅓ cup powdered sugar and ¼ teaspoon salt in medium bowl; cut in butter with pastry blender or fingertips until mixture resembles coarse crumbs. Press mixture evenly onto bottom of prepared pan. Bake 15 minutes.

3 Meanwhile, combine remaining ¼ cup flour, ¼ teaspoon salt, brown sugar, eggs, coconut, pecans and baking powder in medium bowl; mix well. Spread evenly over baked crust; bake 20 minutes. Cool completely in pan on wire rack.

4 For icing, whisk powdered sugar, lemon juice and softened butter in medium bowl until smooth. Spread over bars. Cover and refrigerate until glaze is set. Cut into bars. Store in airtight container in refrigerator.

Toffee Latte Nut Bars

makes 2 to 3 dozen bars

- **1½ cups all-purpose flour**
- **¼ cup powdered sugar or granulated sugar**
- **½ teaspoon salt**
- **¾ cup (1½ sticks) cold butter, cut into small pieces**
- **2 teaspoons instant coffee granules**
- **1 teaspoon hot water**
- **1 can (14 ounces) sweetened condensed milk**
- **1 egg**
- **1 teaspoon vanilla**
- **1 package (8 ounces) toffee baking bits**
- **1 cup chopped walnuts or pecans**
- **1 cup flaked sweetened coconut *or* 2 cups large coconut flakes**

1 Preheat oven to 350°F. Line 13×9-inch baking pan with parchment paper.

2 Whisk flour, powdered sugar and salt in large bowl. Cut in butter with pastry blender or fingertips until mixture resembles coarse crumbs. Press into prepared pan. Bake 15 minutes or until lightly browned around edges.

3 Meanwhile, dissolve coffee granules in hot water in large bowl. Add sweetened condensed milk, egg and vanilla; whisk until well blended. Stir in toffee bits and nuts. Pour over crust; sprinkle with coconut.

4 Bake 25 minutes or until filling is set and coconut is toasted. Cool completely in pan on wire rack. Remove from pan using parchment; cut into bars.

Ultimate Brownie Sundae

makes 9 servings

- ¾ cup (1½ sticks) butter, cut into pieces
- 4 ounces unsweetened chocolate, chopped
- 1¾ cups sugar
- 4 eggs
- 1 teaspoon vanilla
- ¾ cup all-purpose flour
- ½ teaspoon salt
- Hot fudge sauce
- Caramel ice cream topping
- Vanilla ice cream
- ½ cup chopped pecans

1 Preheat oven to 350°F. Line 8-inch square baking pan with parchment paper or spray with nonstick cooking spray.

2 Combine butter and chocolate in medium saucepan; heat over low heat until melted, stirring frequently. Remove from heat; stir in sugar until well blended. Add eggs, one at a time, beating until well blended after each addition. Stir in vanilla. Add flour and salt; stir just until blended. Spread batter in prepared pan.

3 Bake 20 to 23 minutes or until toothpick inserted into center comes out with fudgy crumbs. Cool in pan on wire rack 10 minutes.

4 Heat hot fudge sauce and caramel topping according to package directions. Cut brownie into nine squares. For each serving, place one warm brownie on serving plate; drizzle with hot fudge sauce. Top with ice cream, caramel topping and pecans. Serve immediately.

Red Velvet Brownies

makes 2 to 3 dozen bars

Brownies

- 1 cup (2 sticks) butter
- 2 tablespoons unsweetened cocoa powder
- ½ teaspoon instant espresso powder or coffee granules
- ¼ teaspoon salt
- 1¾ cups granulated sugar
- 4 eggs
- 1 tablespoon red food coloring
- 1 cup all-purpose flour
- 1 cup white chocolate chips

Frosting

- 1 package (8 ounces) cream cheese, softened
- ¼ cup (½ stick) butter, softened
- 4 cups powdered sugar
- 1 to 2 tablespoons milk or cream
- 1 teaspoon vanilla

1 Preheat oven to 350°F. Line 13×9-inch baking pan with parchment paper.

2 Melt 1 cup butter in large saucepan over medium heat. Remove from heat; stir in cocoa, espresso powder and salt. Let stand 5 minutes to cool.

3 Stir granulated sugar into butter mixture until well blended. Add eggs, one at a time, beating well after each addition. Stir in food coloring. Add flour; stir until no white streaks remain. Stir in white chips. Spread batter into prepared pan; smooth top.

4 Bake 30 minutes or until top is firm and toothpick inserted into center comes out clean. Cool completely in pan on wire rack.

5 For frosting, beat cream cheese and ¼ cup butter in large bowl with electric mixer at medium speed until well blended. Add powdered sugar; beat at low speed until combined. Add 1 tablespoon milk and vanilla; beat until blended. Increase speed to medium-high; beat 3 minutes or until light and fluffy, adding additional milk if frosting is too stiff.

6 Spread frosting over cooled brownies. Cover and refrigerate 1 hour or until frosting is firm. Remove from pan using parchment; cut into bars. Store in airtight container in refrigerator.

White Chip Pecan Blondies

makes 12 to 16 bars

1 cup all-purpose flour
½ teaspoon baking powder
½ teaspoon baking soda
½ teaspoon salt
½ cup (1 stick) butter
1 cup packed brown sugar
1 egg
1 tablespoon vanilla
½ cup white chocolate chips
½ cup chopped candied pecans

1 Preheat oven to 350°F. Line 8-inch baking pan with parchment paper. Whisk flour, baking powder, baking soda and salt in large bowl.

2 Melt butter in small saucepan over medium-low heat. Cook 5 to 7 minutes or until butter is browned and smells nutty (watch carefully; butter can brown too quickly at the end). Cool slightly. Stir in brown sugar, egg and vanilla until well blended. Add to flour mixture; stir just until blended. Stir in white chips and pecans. Spread batter in prepared pan.

3 Bake about 20 minutes or until slightly firm on top and edges are golden brown. Cool completely in pan on wire rack. Remove from pan using parchment; cut into bars.

Super Fudgy Brownies

makes 12 to 16 brownies

½ cup all-purpose flour
½ cup unsweetened cocoa powder
½ teaspoon salt
½ cup (1 stick) butter
1 cup sugar
2 eggs
1 teaspoon vanilla
¾ cup semisweet or bittersweet chocolate chips

1 Preheat oven to 350°F. Spray 8-inch square baking pan with nonstick cooking spray. Line with parchment paper, leaving overhang on two sides; spray parchment.

2 Sift flour, cocoa and salt into small bowl. Melt butter in medium saucepan over medium heat. Remove from heat; add sugar and whisk 2 minutes. Add eggs and vanilla; whisk 1 minute or until very well blended. Add flour mixture; stir just until blended. Stir in chocolate chips. Spread batter in prepared pan; smooth top.

3 Bake 20 to 22 minutes or until edges are set and toothpick inserted into center comes out with moist crumbs. Cool completely in pan on wire rack. Remove from pan using parchment; cut into bars.

White Chocolate and Almond Brownies

makes 12 to 16 brownies

- **12 ounces white chocolate, broken into pieces**
- **1 cup (2 sticks) butter**
- **3 eggs**
- **1 teaspoon vanilla**
- **¾ cup all-purpose flour**
- **½ teaspoon salt**
- **½ cup slivered almonds**

1 Preheat oven to 325°F. Grease and flour 9-inch square baking pan.

2 Melt white chocolate and butter in large heavy saucepan over very low heat, stirring constantly. (White chocolate may separate.) Remove from heat when chocolate is just melted. Transfer to large bowl; cool slightly.

3 Add eggs and vanilla; beat with electric mixer at medium speed until smooth. Add flour and salt; beat at low speed just until blended. Spread batter in prepared pan; sprinkle with almonds.

4 Bake 30 minutes or until top is set and toothpick inserted into center comes out clean. Cool completely in pan on wire rack. Cut into bars.

Chocolate Gingerbread Brownies

makes 12 to 16 brownies

Brownies

- ¾ cup all-purpose flour
- ½ cup unsweetened cocoa powder
- 2 teaspoons ground ginger
- 1 teaspoon ground cinnamon
- ½ teaspoon baking powder
- ½ teaspoon salt
- ⅛ teaspoon ground allspice
- ⅛ teaspoon ground cloves
- ⅛ teaspoon ground nutmeg
- ¾ cup (1½ sticks) butter
- ¾ cup packed brown sugar
- ¾ cup granulated sugar
- 3 eggs
- 2 tablespoons molasses
- 1 teaspoon vanilla

Frosting

- ¼ cup (½ stick) butter
- 2 cups powdered sugar
- ¼ cup buttermilk
- 2 tablespoons unsweetened cocoa powder
- 1 teaspoon ground ginger
- ½ teaspoon ground cinnamon
- ½ teaspoon vanilla

1 Preheat oven to 350°F. Spray 8-inch square baking pan with nonstick cooking spray or line with parchment paper. Whisk flour, ½ cup cocoa, 2 teaspoons ginger, 1 teaspoon cinnamon, baking powder, salt, allspice, cloves and nutmeg in large bowl.

2 Melt butter in medium saucepan over low heat. Remove from heat; whisk in brown sugar and granulated sugar until well blended. Add eggs, molasses and 1 teaspoon vanilla; beat until well blended. Add to flour mixture; stir just until blended. Spread batter in prepared pan; smooth top.

3 Bake 35 to 40 minutes or until toothpick inserted into center comes out clean. Cool completely in pan on wire rack.

4 For frosting, melt ¼ cup butter in small saucepan over low heat. Add powdered sugar, buttermilk, 2 tablespoons cocoa, 1 teaspoon ginger, ½ teaspoon cinnamon and ½ teaspoon vanilla; whisk until smooth. Spread evenly over brownies; let stand until set. Cut into bars.

Orange Marmalade Bars

makes 2 to 3 dozen bars

Crust

- ¾ cup hazelnuts
- 1 cup all-purpose flour
- 6 tablespoons cold butter, cut into pieces
- ¼ cup packed brown sugar
- 1 egg
- 1 teaspoon vanilla

Filling

- 1 cup plus 2 teaspoons orange marmalade, divided
- 4 ounces cream cheese, softened
- ¼ cup whipping cream
- 1 tablespoon granulated sugar
- 1 tablespoon grated orange peel

Topping

- 2 tablespoons packed brown sugar
- 2 tablespoons melted butter
- 1 teaspoon all-purpose flour

1 Preheat oven to 375°F. Line 13×19-inch baking pan with parchment paper. Spread nuts on baking sheet. Bake 5 minutes or until lightly browned and fragrant. Place nuts in clean kitchen towel; roll in towel to remove skins.

2 For crust, process ¼ cup hazelnuts in food processor until finely chopped. Add flour; pulse until blended. Add butter and brown sugar; pulse until mixture resembles coarse crumbs. Add egg and vanilla; process just until dough forms.

3 Press dough evenly into prepared pan. Bake 12 to 15 minutes or until crust is golden brown. Spread 1 cup marmalade over hot crust.

4 For filling, beat cream cheese, cream, granulated sugar, remaining 2 teaspoons marmalade and orange peel in large bowl with electric mixer at medium speed until smooth and creamy.

5 For topping, finely chop remaining ½ cup nuts. Combine nuts, brown sugar, melted butter and 1 teaspoon flour in small bowl until nuts are evenly coated. Spread filling over marmalade; sprinkle with topping.

6 Bake 12 to 15 minutes or until topping is lightly browned and filling bubbles slightly. Cool completely in pan on wire rack. Remove from pan using parchment; cut into bars. Store in airtight container in refrigerator.

Cakes & Cupcakes

Apple Ring Coffeecake

makes 12 servings

- 3 cups all-purpose flour
- 1 teaspoon baking soda
- 1 teaspoon salt
- 1 teaspoon ground cinnamon
- 1 cup chopped walnuts
- 1½ cups granulated sugar
- 1 cup vegetable oil
- 2 eggs
- 2 teaspoons vanilla
- 2 medium tart apples, peeled and chopped
- Powdered sugar (optional)

1 Preheat oven to 325°F. Spray 10-inch tube pan with nonstick cooking spray.

2 Whisk flour, baking soda, salt and cinnamon in large bowl. Stir in walnuts. Combine granulated sugar, oil, eggs and vanilla in medium bowl; mix well. Stir in apples. Add to flour mixture; stir just until blended. Spread batter evenly in prepared pan.

3 Bake 1 hour or until toothpick inserted near center comes out clean. Cool in pan on wire rack 10 minutes. Loosen edges with metal spatula, if necessary. Remove to wire rack; cool completely.

4 Sprinkle with powdered sugar just before serving, if desired.

Devil's Food Cake

makes 12 to 16 servings

- 2 cups cake flour
- ½ cup unsweetened cocoa powder
- 2 teaspoons baking powder
- ½ teaspoon baking soda
- ½ teaspoon salt
- 6 tablespoons butter, softened
- 1½ cups granulated sugar
- 3 eggs
- 1½ teaspoons vanilla
- 1 cup buttermilk*
- Creamy Chocolate Frosting (page 55)

**If buttermilk is unavailable, substitute 1 tablespoon vinegar or lemon juice and enough milk to equal 1 cup. Stir; let stand 5 minutes.*

1 Preheat oven to 350°F. Grease and flour three 8-inch round cake pans.

2 Whisk flour, cocoa, baking powder, baking soda and salt in medium bowl. Beat butter and granulated sugar in large bowl with electric mixer at medium speed until light and fluffy. Add eggs, one at a time, beating until blended after each addition. Beat in vanilla. Add flour mixture alternately with buttermilk, beating at low speed just until blended. Divide batter evenly among prepared pans.

3 Bake 25 to 30 minutes or until toothpick inserted into centers comes out clean. Cool in pans 10 minutes. Remove to wire racks; cool completely.

4 Meanwhile, prepare Creamy Chocolate Frosting. Place one cake layer on serving plate; spread with frosting. Repeat with remaining two cake layers and frosting. Frost side and top of cake.

Creamy Chocolate Frosting

makes about 2½ cups frosting

½ cup (1 stick) butter, softened
5 cups powdered sugar
½ cup unsweetened cocoa powder
6 tablespoons milk
1 teaspoon vanilla

1 Beat butter in large bowl with electric mixer at medium speed until creamy. Gradually add powdered sugar and cocoa, beating until smooth.

2 Add milk and vanilla; beat at medium-high speed about 5 minutes or until light and fluffy.

Butter Pecan Cupcakes

makes 30 cupcakes

- **2 cups chopped pecans**
- **3 cups all-purpose flour**
- **2 teaspoons baking powder**
- **½ teaspoon salt**
- **¾ cup milk**
- **¼ cup vegetable oil**
- **1½ teaspoons vanilla**
- **2 cups granulated sugar**
- **1 cup (2 sticks) butter, softened**
- **4 eggs**
- **Browned Butter Frosting (page 57)**
- **Whole pecans (optional)**

1 Preheat oven to 350°F. Line 30 standard (2½-inch) muffin cups with paper baking cups.

2 Spread chopped pecans in shallow baking pan. Bake 5 minutes or until lightly toasted, stirring occasionally. Transfer to plate; cool completely.

3 Whisk flour, baking powder and salt in medium bowl. Combine milk, oil and vanilla in small bowl. Beat granulated sugar and butter in large bowl with electric mixer at medium speed until creamy. Add eggs, one at a time, beating well after each addition. Add flour mixture alternately with milk mixture, beating at low speed just until blended. Stir in chopped pecans. Spoon batter evenly into prepared muffin cups.

4 Bake 20 minutes or until toothpick inserted into centers comes out clean. Cool in pans 10 minutes. Remove to wire racks; cool completely.

5 Meanwhile, prepare Browned Butter Frosting. Pipe or spread frosting on cupcakes. Garnish with whole pecans.

Browned Butter Frosting

makes about 4 cups frosting

1 cup (2 sticks) butter
5½ cups powdered sugar
¼ cup milk
1½ teaspoons vanilla
¼ teaspoon salt

1 Melt butter in small saucepan over medium heat. Cook 5 to 10 minutes or until butter is light brown and smells nutty, swirling pan occasionally. Pour into large bowl; cool to room temperature.

2 Add powdered sugar, milk, vanilla and salt; beat with electric mixer at medium-high speed 5 minutes or until light and fluffy.

Lemon Pound Cake

makes 12 servings

Cake

- 1 cup (2 sticks) plus 2 tablespoons butter, softened, divided
- 3 cups all-purpose flour
- 1 teaspoon baking powder
- 1 teaspoon salt
- 2½ cups granulated sugar
- 5 eggs, at room temperature
- ½ cup lemon juice
- 1 tablespoon grated lemon peel
- 2 teaspoons vanilla
- 1 cup sour cream

Glaze

- 2 tablespoons butter
- 2 cups powdered sugar
- 2 tablespoons lemon juice

1 Preheat oven to 350°F. Generously grease 12-cup (10-inch) bundt pan with 2 tablespoons butter and dust with flour. Whisk flour, baking powder and salt in small bowl.

2 Beat remaining 1 cup butter in large bowl with electric mixer at medium speed until creamy. Gradually add granulated sugar; beat at medium-high speed 3 minutes or until light and fluffy. Scrape bowl. Add eggs, one at a time, beating until well blended after each addition. Beat in ½ cup lemon juice, lemon peel and vanilla. Stop and scrape bowl. Add flour mixture alternately with sour cream, beating at low speed just until blended. Spread batter in prepared pan.

3 Bake 1 hour 5 minutes or until wooden skewer inserted near center comes out with a few moist crumbs. Cool in pan on wire rack 10 minutes. Invert onto wire rack; cool completely.

4 For glaze, melt 2 tablespoons butter in small saucepan. Whisk in powdered sugar and 2 tablespoons lemon juice until smooth. Cook 1 minute, whisking constantly. Pour over cake.

Salted Caramel Cupcakes

makes 12 cupcakes

- 1½ cups all-purpose flour
- 1 teaspoon baking powder
- ½ teaspoon salt
- 1 cup packed brown sugar
- ½ cup (1 stick) butter, softened
- 2 eggs
- 1 teaspoon vanilla
- ½ cup buttermilk
- Salted Caramel Frosting (page 61)
- Flaky sea salt

1 Preheat oven to 325°F. Line 12 standard (2½-inch) muffin cups with paper baking cups. Whisk flour, baking powder and ½ teaspoon salt in small bowl.

2 Beat brown sugar and butter in large bowl with electric mixer at medium speed until light and fluffy. Add eggs and vanilla; beat until well blended. Add flour mixture alternately with buttermilk, beating at low speed just until blended. Spoon batter evenly into prepared muffin cups.

3 Bake 20 to 25 minutes or until toothpick inserted into centers comes out clean. Cool in pan 10 minutes. Remove to wire rack; cool completely.

4 Prepare Salted Caramel Frosting. Pipe or spread frosting on cupcakes; sprinkle lightly with sea salt.

Salted Caramel Frosting

½ cup granulated sugar
2 tablespoons water
¼ cup whipping cream
½ teaspoon salt
1 cup (2 sticks) butter, softened
2½ cups powdered sugar

1 Combine granulated sugar and water in heavy medium saucepan. Cook over high heat, without stirring, until medium to dark amber in color. Remove from heat; carefully stir in cream and salt (mixture will foam). Cool 15 minutes.

2 Beat butter and caramel mixture in large bowl with electric mixer at medium-high speed until well blended. Add powdered sugar; beat until thick and creamy. (If frosting is too soft, refrigerate 10 minutes.)

Cannoli Cake

makes 12 to 16 servings

Cake

- 2½ cups all-purpose flour
- 1 tablespoon baking powder
- 1 teaspoon baking soda
- 1 teaspoon salt
- 1¼ cups buttermilk
- ½ cup vegetable oil
- 1½ teaspoons vanilla
- 1½ cups granulated sugar
- ½ cup (1 stick) butter, softened
- 3 eggs

Frosting

- 2 cups (16 ounces) mascarpone cheese
- ½ cup ricotta cheese
- ¼ cup (½ stick) butter, softened
- Grated peel of 1 orange
- 1 teaspoon vanilla
- Pinch of salt
- 5 to 6 cups powdered sugar
- 1 cup mini chocolate chips
- Mini cannoli (optional)

1 Preheat oven to 350°F. Grease and flour three 8-inch round cake pans.

2 For cake, whisk flour, baking powder, baking soda and 1 teaspoon salt in medium bowl. Whisk buttermilk, oil and 1½ teaspoons vanilla in medium bowl until blended. Beat granulated sugar and ½ cup butter in large bowl with electric mixer at medium speed about 5 minutes or until light and fluffy. Add eggs, one at a time, beating until blended after each addition. Add flour mixture alternately with buttermilk mixture in three additions, beating at low speed just until blended. Divide batter evenly among prepared pans.

3 Bake 25 to 30 minutes or until toothpick inserted into centers comes out clean. Cool in pans 10 minutes. Remove to wire racks; cool completely.

4 For frosting, beat mascarpone, ricotta and ¼ cup butter in large bowl with electric mixer at medium speed until well blended and smooth. Beat in orange peel, 1 teaspoon vanilla and pinch of salt. Gradually add 5 cups powdered sugar; beat until well blended. Add additional powdered sugar, ¼ cup at a time, if necessary to reach spreading consistency.

5 Place one cake layer on serving plate. Spread with 1 cup frosting; sprinkle with 2 tablespoons chocolate chips. Top with second cake layer; spread with 1 cup frosting and sprinkle with 2 tablespoons chocolate chips. Top with remaining cake layer; spread remaining frosting over top and side of cake. Press remaining chocolate chips into side of cake. Refrigerate 6 hours or overnight. Garnish with mini cannoli just before serving.

Cinnamon Swirl Coffeecake

makes 9 to 12 servings

Filling and Topping

- ⅓ cup all-purpose flour
- ⅓ cup granulated sugar
- ⅓ cup packed brown sugar
- 1½ tablespoons ground cinnamon
- ¼ teaspoon salt
- ⅛ teaspoon ground allspice
- 3 tablespoons melted butter

Cake

- 2 cups all-purpose flour
- 1½ teaspoons baking powder
- ¾ teaspoon baking soda
- ½ teaspoon salt
- 9 tablespoons butter, softened
- 1¼ cups granulated sugar
- 3 eggs
- ½ cup sour cream
- 2 teaspoons vanilla
- ¾ cup milk

1 Preheat oven to 350°F. Spray 9-inch square baking pan with nonstick cooking spray.

2 For filling, combine ⅓ cup flour, ⅓ cup granulated sugar, brown sugar, cinnamon, ¼ teaspoon salt and allspice in small bowl; mix well. For topping, remove half of mixture to another small bowl; stir in melted butter until blended.

3 For cake, whisk 2 cups flour, baking powder, baking soda and ½ teaspoon salt in medium bowl. Combine 9 tablespoons butter and 1¼ cups granulated sugar in large bowl; beat with electric mixer at medium speed 3 minutes or until light and fluffy. Add eggs, sour cream and vanilla; beat until well blended. Scrape down side of bowl. Add flour mixture alternately with milk in two additions, beating at low speed until blended. Spread half of batter in prepared pan; sprinkle evenly with filling. Spread remaining batter over filling with dampened hands. Sprinkle with topping.

4 Bake 45 to 50 minutes or until toothpick inserted into center comes out clean. Cool completely in pan on wire rack.

Vanilla-Strawberry Cupcakes

makes 28 cupcakes

- **2 cups all-purpose flour**
- **2 teaspoons baking powder**
- **¼ teaspoon salt**
- **1¾ cups granulated sugar**
- **¾ cup (1½ sticks) butter, softened, divided**
- **3½ teaspoons vanilla, divided**
- **¾ cup milk**
- **3 egg whites**
- **½ cup strawberry preserves**
- **1 package (8 ounces) cold cream cheese, cut into pieces**
- **2 cups powdered sugar**
- **1 to 1½ cups sliced fresh strawberries**

1 Preheat oven to 350°F. Grease 28 standard (2½-inch) muffin cups or line with paper baking cups.

2 Whisk flour, baking powder and salt in medium bowl. Beat granulated sugar, ½ cup butter and 1½ teaspoons vanilla in large bowl with electric mixer at medium speed 1 minute. Add flour mixture alternately with milk, beating just until blended. Add egg whites; beat 1 minute.

3 Spoon batter into prepared muffin cups, filling half full. Drop 1 teaspoon preserves on top of batter in each cup; swirl into batter with toothpick.

4 Bake 18 to 20 minutes or until toothpick inserted into centers comes out clean. Cool in pans 10 minutes. Remove to wire racks; cool completely. (At this point, cupcakes may be frozen up to 3 months. Thaw at room temperature before frosting.)

5 Combine cream cheese, remaining ¼ cup butter and 2 teaspoons vanilla in food processor; process just until blended. Add powdered sugar; pulse just until sugar is incorporated. (Do not overmix or frosting will be too soft.)

6 Frost cupcakes. Top with strawberries just before serving.

Chocolate Overload Cake

makes 12 to 16 servings

- 4 cups all-purpose flour
- 4 cups sugar
- 1½ cups unsweetened cocoa powder
- 3½ teaspoons baking soda
- 1 tablespoon baking powder
- 2⅛ teaspoons salt, divided
- 4 eggs
- 2 cups buttermilk
- 1 cup vegetable oil
- 4 teaspoons vanilla
- 2 cups very hot coffee
- 6¾ cups semisweet chocolate chips, divided
- 3 cups whipping cream
- ¼ cup light corn syrup
- 2 cups chopped walnuts

1 Preheat oven to 350°F. Spray bottoms of three 9-inch round cake pans lightly with nonstick cooking spray; line with parchment paper. Spray bottoms and sides of pans with baking spray or grease and flour pans.

2 Whisk flour, sugar, cocoa, baking soda, baking powder and 2 teaspoons salt in large bowl of electric mixer. Whisk eggs in medium bowl. Add buttermilk, oil and vanilla; whisk until well blended. Gradually add egg mixture to flour mixture (mixer will be very full), beating at low speed until blended. Beat at medium speed 2 minutes. Gradually add coffee, beating at low speed until blended. (Batter will be thin.) Divide batter evenly among prepared pans. Sprinkle each layer with ¼ cup chocolate chips.

3 Bake about 45 minutes or until toothpick inserted into centers comes out clean. (Rotate cake pans top to bottom and left to right halfway through baking.) Cool in pans 10 minutes. Remove to wire racks; cool completely.

4 Combine cream, corn syrup and remaining ⅛ teaspoon salt in large saucepan; heat over medium heat just until mixture begins to bubble. Add remaining 6 cups chocolate chips; let stand 3 minutes. Whisk until well blended and smooth. Remove half of filling (about 4 cups) to medium bowl; refrigerate 30 minutes to 1 hour or until thick and spreadable. (Leave remaining mixture at room temperature to frost top and side of cake.)

5 Cut each cake layer in half horizontally with long serrated knife. Place one bottom cake layer, cut side up, on serving plate; spread with chilled filling (about ⅔ cup per layer). Top with second top cake layer, cut side up; spread with filling. Repeat with remaining cake layers and chilled filling until final cake layer is reached. Place top layer cut side down over filling.

6 Microwave remaining chocolate mixture on LOW (30%) 2 to 3 minutes or just until pourable, stirring after each minute. Pour frosting over top of cake so it runs down side; use long metal spatula to smooth frosting around side of cake. Refrigerate 10 minutes or until frosting is partially set. Gently press walnuts into side of cake.

Toffee Cake with Whiskey Sauce

makes 9 servings

- **8 ounces chopped dates**
- **2¼ teaspoons baking soda, divided**
- **1½ cups boiling water**
- **2 cups all-purpose flour**
- **½ teaspoon salt**
- **¾ cup (1½ sticks) butter, softened**
- **½ cup granulated sugar**
- **½ cup packed dark brown sugar**
- **2 eggs**
- **1 teaspoon vanilla**
- **1½ cups butterscotch sauce**
- **2 tablespoons whiskey**
- **1 cup glazed pecans* or chopped toasted pecans**
- **Vanilla ice cream**

Glazed or candied pecans may be found in the produce section of the supermarket with other salad toppings, or they may be found in the snack aisle.

1 Preheat oven to 350°F. Spray 9-inch square baking pan with nonstick cooking spray.

2 Combine dates and 1½ teaspoons baking soda in medium bowl. Stir in boiling water; let stand 10 minutes to soften. Mash with fork or process in food processor until mixture forms paste.

3 Whisk flour, remaining ¾ teaspoon baking soda and salt in medium bowl. Beat butter, granulated sugar and brown sugar in large bowl with electric mixer at medium speed 3 minutes or until creamy. Add eggs, one at a time, beating well after each addition. Beat in vanilla. Add flour mixture alternately with date mixture, beating at low speed just until blended. Spread batter in prepared pan.

4 Bake about 30 minutes or until toothpick inserted into center comes out with moist crumbs. Cool in pan on wire rack 15 minutes.

5 Pour butterscotch sauce into medium microwavable bowl; microwave on HIGH 30 seconds or until warm. Stir in whiskey. Drizzle sauce over each serving; sprinkle with pecans and top with ice cream.

Chocolate Hazelnut Delight

makes 12 to 16 servings

- 1 package (2¼ ounces) chopped hazelnuts
- 2 cups cake flour
- ½ cup unsweetened cocoa powder
- 1½ teaspoons baking soda
- 1 teaspoon baking powder
- 1 teaspoon salt
- 1 cup (2 sticks) butter, softened
- 1 cup packed brown sugar
- ½ cup granulated sugar
- 3 eggs
- 4 ounces unsweetened chocolate, melted
- 1 teaspoon vanilla
- 1 cup milk
- ½ cup warm water
- Chocolate Hazelnut Frosting (page 75)
- Whole toasted hazelnuts (optional)

1 For cake, preheat oven to 350°F. Spray three 9-inch round cake pans with nonstick cooking spray. Line bottoms with parchment paper; spray parchment. Spread chopped hazelnuts on baking sheet. Bake 7 minutes or until lightly browned and fragrant.

2 Whisk flour, cocoa, baking soda, baking powder and salt in medium bowl. Stir in chopped hazelnuts.

3 Beat 1 cup butter, brown sugar and granulated sugar in large bowl with electric mixer at medium speed about 5 minutes or until light and fluffy. Add eggs, one at a time, beating well after each addition. Beat in melted chocolate and 1 teaspoon vanilla. Add flour mixture alternately with milk, beating at low speed just until blended. Stir in water. Divide batter between prepared pans.

4 Bake 30 minutes or until toothpick inserted into centers comes out clean. Cool in pans 10 minutes. Remove from pans; peel off parchment. Cool completely on wire rack.

5 Meanwhile, prepare frosting. Place one cake layer on serving plate and spread with frosting. Repeat with remaining cake layers. Frost top and side of cake. Pipe 16 rosettes around cake; top with whole hazelnuts, if desired.

Chocolate Hazelnut Frosting

makes about 3 cups frosting

- **1 cup (2 sticks) butter, softened**
- **4 cups powdered sugar**
- **¼ cup milk**
- **1 teaspoon vanilla**
- **1 jar (13 ounces) chocolate hazelnut spread**

1 Beat butter in large bowl with electric at medium speed until creamy. Beat in powdered sugar until light and fluffy; beat in milk and vanilla.

2 Add chocolate hazelnut spread; beat at medium-high speed 5 minutes or until light and fluffy.

Pies, Cobblers & Crisps

Summer Berry Sugar Cookie Cobbler

makes 12 servings

4 cups sliced fresh strawberries
4 cups fresh blueberries
3 cups fresh blackberries
¾ cup sugar
3½ tablespoons cornstarch
½ teaspoon ground cinnamon
12 ready-to-bake refrigerated sugar cookies (half of 16-ounce package)*

Reserve remaining half of package for another use.

1 Preheat oven to 350°F.

2 Combine berries, sugar, cornstarch and cinnamon in large bowl; toss gently to coat. Spoon into 13×9-inch baking dish.

3 Bake 10 minutes. Remove from oven; crumble cookie dough over fruit mixture. Bake 45 to 50 minutes or until filling is bubbly and cookie dough is crisp and golden brown.

Chocolate Walnut Toffee Tart

makes 12 servings

- **2 cups all-purpose flour**
- **1¼ cups plus 3 tablespoons sugar, divided**
- **¾ cup (1½ sticks) cold butter, cut into pieces**
- **2 egg yolks**
- **1¼ cups whipping cream**
- **1 teaspoon ground cinnamon**
- **2 teaspoons vanilla**
- **2 cups coarsely chopped walnuts**
- **1¼ cups semisweet chocolate chips or chunks, divided**

1 Preheat oven to 325°F. Line baking sheet with foil.

2 Combine flour and 3 tablespoons sugar in food processor; pulse just until blended. Scatter butter over flour mixture; process 20 seconds. Add egg yolks; process 10 seconds (mixture may be crumbly).

3 Press dough firmly into ungreased 10-inch tart pan with removable bottom or 9- or 10-inch pie plate. Bake 10 minutes or until surface is no longer shiny. Place tart pan on prepared baking sheet. *Increase oven temperature to 375°F.*

4 Combine remaining 1¼ cups sugar, cream and cinnamon in large saucepan; bring to a boil over medium-high heat. Reduce heat to medium-low; simmer 10 minutes, stirring frequently. Remove from heat; stir in vanilla. Sprinkle walnuts and 1 cup chocolate chips evenly over crust. Pour cream mixture over top.

5 Bake 35 to 40 minutes or until filling is bubbly and crust is lightly browned. Cool completely on wire rack.

6 Place remaining ¼ cup chocolate chips in small resealable food storage bag. Microwave on HIGH 20 seconds; knead bag until chocolate is melted. Cut small hole in one corner of bag; drizzle chocolate over tart.

Note: Tart may be made up to 5 days in advance. Cover with plastic wrap and store at room temperature.

Banana Cream Pie

makes 8 servings

- 1 refrigerated pie crust (half of 14-ounce package), at room temperature
- ⅔ cup sugar
- ¼ cup cornstarch
- ¼ teaspoon salt
- 2½ cups milk
- 4 egg yolks, beaten
- 2 tablespoons butter, softened
- 2 teaspoons vanilla
- 2 medium bananas
- 1 teaspoon lemon juice
- Whipped cream and toasted sliced almonds (optional)

1 Preheat oven to 400°F. Line 9-inch pie plate with crust; flute edge. Prick bottom and side all over with fork. Bake 10 minutes or until crust is golden brown. Cool completely on wire rack.

2 Combine sugar, cornstarch and salt in medium saucepan; whisk in milk until well blended. Cook over medium heat about 12 minutes or until mixture boils and thickens, stirring constantly. Boil 2 minutes, stirring constantly. Remove from heat.

3 Gradually whisk ½ cup hot milk mixture into egg yolks in small bowl. Gradually whisk mixture back into milk mixture in saucepan. Cook over medium heat about 5 minutes, whisking constantly. Remove from heat; whisk in butter and vanilla. Cool 20 minutes, stirring occasionally. Strain through fine-mesh strainer into medium bowl. Press plastic wrap onto surface of pudding; cool about 30 minutes or until lukewarm.

4 Cut bananas into ¼-inch slices; toss with lemon juice in medium bowl. Spread half of pudding in cooled crust; arrange bananas over pudding. (Reserve several slices for garnish, if desired.) Spread remaining pudding over bananas. Refrigerate 4 hours or overnight. Garnish with whipped cream, almonds and reserved banana slices.

Fresh Fruit Tart

makes 8 servings

- **1⅔ cups all-purpose flour**
- **⅓ cup sugar**
- **¼ teaspoon salt**
- **½ cup (1 stick) butter, softened and cut into pieces**
- **1 egg yolk**
- **2 to 3 tablespoons milk**
- **1 package (8 ounces) cream cheese, softened**
- **⅓ cup strawberry jam**
- **2 to 3 cups mixed assorted fresh fruit, such as sliced bananas, sliced kiwi, blueberries, sliced peaches, sliced plums, raspberries and halved strawberries**
- **¼ cup apple jelly, melted**

1 Combine flour, sugar and salt in food processor; process until just combined. Add butter; pulse until mixture resembles coarse crumbs. Add egg yolk and 2 tablespoons milk; process until dough leaves side of bowl. Add additional milk by teaspoons, if necessary. Shape dough into a disc. Wrap in plastic wrap and refrigerate 30 minutes or until firm.

2 Preheat oven to 350°F. Roll out dough ¼ inch thick into 12-inch circle on lightly floured surface. Transfer to 10-inch tart pan with removable bottom; press dough lightly onto bottom and up side of pan. Trim edge even with edge of pan. Bake 16 to 18 minutes or until light golden brown. Cool completely in pan on wire rack.

3 Combine cream cheese and strawberry jam in small bowl; mix well. Spread evenly over cooled crust. Arrange fruit decoratively over cream cheese layer. Brush fruit with apple jelly. Serve immediately or refrigerate up to 2 hours before serving.

Warm Apple Crostata

makes 4 tarts (4 to 8 servings)

- **1¾ cups all-purpose flour**
- **⅓ cup granulated sugar**
- **½ teaspoon plus ⅛ teaspoon salt, divided**
- **¾ cup (1½ sticks) cold butter, cut into pieces**
- **3 tablespoons ice water**
- **2 teaspoons vanilla**
- **4 Pink Lady or Honeycrisp apples (about 1½ pounds), peeled and cut into ¼-inch slices**
- **¼ cup packed brown sugar**
- **1 tablespoon lemon juice**
- **1 teaspoon ground cinnamon**
- **⅛ teaspoon ground nutmeg**
- **4 teaspoons butter, cut into very small pieces**
- **1 egg, beaten**
- **1 to 2 teaspoons coarse sugar**
- **Vanilla ice cream**
- **Caramel sauce**

1. Combine flour, granulated sugar and ½ teaspoon salt in food processor; process 5 seconds. Add ¾ cup cold butter; process 10 seconds or until mixture resembles coarse crumbs.

2. Combine ice water and vanilla in small bowl. With motor running, pour mixture through feed tube; process 12 seconds or until dough begins to come together. Shape dough into a disc; wrap in plastic wrap and refrigerate 30 minutes.

3. Meanwhile, combine apples, brown sugar, lemon juice, cinnamon, nutmeg and remaining ⅛ teaspoon salt in large bowl; toss to coat. Preheat oven to 400°F.

4. Line two large baking sheets with parchment paper. Cut dough into four pieces; roll out each piece into 7-inch circle on floured surface. Place on prepared baking sheets; mound apples in center of dough circles (about 1 cup apples for each crostata). Fold or roll up edges of dough towards center to create rim of crostata. Dot apples with 4 teaspoons butter. Brush dough with egg; sprinkle dough and apples with coarse sugar.

5 Bake 20 minutes or until apples are tender and crust is golden brown. Serve warm topped with ice cream and caramel sauce.

Strawberries and Cream Cobbler

makes 6 servings

- 2 pounds fresh strawberries, hulled and sliced
- ½ cup strawberry jam
- ⅔ cup all-purpose flour
- ⅓ cup sugar
- 1 teaspoon baking powder
- ¼ teaspoon salt
- 2 tablespoons cold butter
- ¼ cup milk
- 6 tablespoons whipping cream

1 Preheat oven to 375°F. Spray six 8-ounce ramekins or custard cups with nonstick cooking spray. Place on baking sheet.

2 Combine strawberries and jam in large skillet; cook over medium heat 20 minutes or until thickened and reduced, stirring occasionally.

3 Meanwhile, whisk flour, sugar, baking powder and salt in medium bowl. Cut in butter with pastry blender or fingertips until mixture resembles fine crumbs. Stir in milk to make soft dough.

4 Divide strawberry mixture evenly among prepared ramekins. Spoon dough evenly over strawberry mixture, spreading with back of spoon.

5 Bake 20 to 25 minutes or until crust is golden brown. Serve warm; drizzle each cobbler with 1 tablespoon cream.

Apple-Pear Praline Pie

makes 8 servings

- Double-Crust Pie Pastry (recipe follows)
- 4 cups sliced peeled Granny Smith apples
- 2 cups sliced peeled pears
- ¾ cup granulated sugar
- ¼ cup plus 1 tablespoon all-purpose flour, divided
- 4 teaspoons ground cinnamon
- ¼ teaspoon salt
- ½ cup (1 stick) plus 2 tablespoons butter, divided
- 1 cup packed brown sugar
- 1 tablespoon half-and-half or milk
- 1 cup chopped pecans

1 Prepare Double-Crust Pie Pastry.

2 Combine apples, pears, granulated sugar, ¼ cup flour, cinnamon and salt in large bowl; toss to coat. Let stand 15 minutes.

3 Preheat oven to 350°F. Roll out one disc of pastry into 11-inch circle on floured surface. Line deep-dish 9-inch pie plate with pastry; sprinkle with remaining 1 tablespoon flour. Spoon apple and pear mixture into crust; dot with 2 tablespoons butter. Roll out remaining disc of pastry into 10-inch circle. Place over fruit; seal and flute edge. Cut slits in top to vent.

4 Bake 1 hour. Meanwhile, combine remaining ½ cup butter, brown sugar and half-and-half in small saucepan; bring to a boil over medium heat, stirring frequently. Boil 2 minutes, stirring constantly. Remove from heat; stir in pecans. Spread over pie.

5 Cool on wire rack 15 minutes. Serve warm or at room temperature.

Double-Crust Pie Pastry: Combine 2½ cups all-purpose flour, 1 teaspoon granulated sugar and 1 teaspoon salt in large bowl. Cut in 1 cup (2 sticks) cold cubed butter with pastry blender or fingertips until coarse crumbs form. Drizzle ⅓ cup ice water over flour mixture, 2 tablespoons at a time, stirring just until dough comes together. Divide dough in half. Shape each half into a disc; wrap in plastic wrap. Refrigerate 30 minutes.

Bananas Foster Crisp

makes 8 to 10 servings

- **¾ cup packed dark brown sugar, divided**
- **6 tablespoons butter, divided**
- **3 tablespoons dark rum**
- **½ teaspoon ground cinnamon**
- **¼ teaspoon ground nutmeg**
- **8 medium bananas (firm, yellow, no spots), cut into ½-inch slices (about 6 cups)**
- **½ cup all-purpose flour**
- **½ cup chopped pecans**
- **¼ teaspoon salt**
- **Vanilla ice cream (optional)**

1 Place oven rack in lower-middle position. Preheat oven to 375°F. Spray 8-inch round or square baking dish with nonstick cooking spray.

2 Combine ½ cup brown sugar and 2 tablespoons butter in small saucepan; cook and stir over medium heat about 3 minutes or until butter is melted and sugar is dissolved. Slowly add rum, cinnamon and nutmeg (mixture will spatter); cook 1 minute, stirring constantly. Pour mixture into large bowl. Add bananas; toss to coat. Spoon into prepared baking dish.

3 Whisk flour, pecans, remaining ¼ cup brown sugar and salt in medium bowl. Cut remaining 4 tablespoons butter into small pieces. Add to flour mixture; mix with fingertips until mixture forms coarse crumbs. Sprinkle over banana mixture.

4 Bake 40 minutes or until filling is bubbly and topping is golden brown. Let stand 1 hour before serving. Serve with ice cream, if desired.

Key Lime Pie

makes 8 servings

12 whole graham crackers*
⅓ cup butter, melted
3 tablespoons sugar
2 cans (14 ounces each) sweetened condensed milk
¾ cup Key lime juice
6 egg yolks
Pinch salt
Whipped cream (optional)
Lime slices (optional)

Or substitute 1½ cups graham cracker crumbs.

1 Preheat oven to 350°F. Spray 9-inch pie plate or springform pan with nonstick cooking spray.

2 Place graham crackers in food processor; pulse until coarse crumbs form. Add butter and sugar; pulse until well blended. Press mixture evenly onto bottom and 1 inch up side of prepared pie plate. Bake 8 minutes or until lightly browned. Remove to wire rack; cool 10 minutes. *Reduce oven temperature to 325°F.*

3 Meanwhile, beat sweetened condensed milk, lime juice, egg yolks and salt in large bowl with electric mixer at medium-low speed 1 minute or until well blended and smooth. Pour mixture over crust.

4 Bake 20 minutes or until top is set. Cool completely on wire rack. Cover; refrigerate 2 hours or overnight. Garnish with whipped cream and lime slices.

Fig-Strawberry Cobbler

makes 6 to 8 servings

Filling

- 1½ pounds fresh strawberries, hulled and quartered
- 1 pound fresh or thawed frozen figs, stemmed and quartered
- ⅓ cup packed brown sugar
- 2 tablespoons cornstarch
- 2 teaspoons grated lemon peel

Dumplings

- 1 cup all-purpose flour
- 1 teaspoon baking powder
- ¼ teaspoon salt
- 1 package (8 ounces) cream cheese, softened
- 5 tablespoons granulated sugar, divided
- ½ cup plus 2 tablespoons milk
- 1 teaspoon vanilla

1. Preheat oven to 350°F. Spray 9-inch round or square baking dish with nonstick cooking spray.

2. Combine strawberries, figs, brown sugar, cornstarch and lemon peel in medium bowl; toss to coat. Spoon into prepared baking dish.

3. Whisk flour, baking powder and salt in medium bowl. Beat cream cheese and 3 tablespoons granulated sugar in large bowl with electric mixer at high speed until light and fluffy. Add milk and vanilla; beat at medium speed until well blended. Add flour mixture; stir just until moistened. Drop by rounded tablespoonfuls onto fruit mixture; sprinkle with remaining 2 tablespoons granulated sugar.

4. Bake in center of oven 55 to 60 minutes or until filling is thick and bubbly and dumplings are browned. Let stand 30 minutes before serving.

Quick Breads

Applesauce Spice Bread

makes 9 to 12 servings

- 1½ cups all-purpose flour
- 1 cup unsweetened applesauce
- ¾ cup packed brown sugar
- ¼ cup shortening or butter
- 1 egg
- 1 teaspoon vanilla
- ¾ teaspoon baking soda
- ¾ teaspoon ground cinnamon
- ¼ teaspoon baking powder
- ¼ teaspoon salt
- ¼ teaspoon ground nutmeg
- ½ cup toasted chopped walnuts
- ½ cup raisins (optional)
- Powdered sugar

1 Preheat oven to 350°F. Spray 9-inch square baking pan with nonstick cooking spray.

2 Combine flour, applesauce, brown sugar, shortening, egg, vanilla, baking soda, cinnamon, baking powder, salt and nutmeg in large bowl; beat with electric mixer at low speed 30 seconds. Beat at high speed 3 minutes. Stir in walnuts and raisins, if desired. Pour batter into prepared pan.

3 Bake 30 minutes or until toothpick inserted into center comes out clean. Cool completely in pan on wire rack. Sprinkle with powdered sugar just before serving.

Glazed Espresso Chocolate Marble Bread

makes 3 loaves

- 4 cups all-purpose flour
- 2 teaspoons baking powder
- 1 teaspoon baking soda
- ½ teaspoon salt
- 1½ cups (3 sticks) butter, softened
- 2 cups sugar
- 4 eggs
- 1 tablespoon vanilla
- 2 cups sour cream
- 1 tablespoon plus ½ teaspoon instant espresso powder or instant coffee powder, divided
- 5 tablespoons hot water, divided
- ¼ cup unsweetened cocoa powder
- ½ cup semisweet chocolate chips
- ¼ cup whipping cream

1. Preheat oven to 350°F. Spray three 8×4-inch loaf pans with nonstick cooking spray.*
2. Whisk flour, baking powder, baking soda and salt in medium bowl. Beat butter in large bowl with electric mixer until creamy. Add sugar; beat until light and fluffy. Add eggs, one at a time, beating well after each addition. Beat in vanilla. Add flour mixture alternately with sour cream, beating at low speed just until blended.
3. Remove half of batter to medium bowl. Stir 1 tablespoon espresso powder into 2 tablespoons hot water until smooth; add to one bowl of batter and mix well. Stir cocoa into remaining 3 tablespoons water until smooth; stir into remaining bowl of batter until well blended. Drop large spoonfuls of both batters alternately into prepared loaf pans. Swirl through batter once or twice with skewer or tip of knife.
4. Bake 45 to 50 minutes or until toothpick inserted into centers comes out clean. Cool in pans 10 minutes. Remove to wire racks; cool completely.

5 Combine chocolate chips, cream and remaining ½ teaspoon espresso powder in small saucepan. Cook over low heat, stirring constantly until melted and smooth. Drizzle glaze over tops of loaves.

**Disposable foil pans are a great solution if you do not have three loaf pans. You can also use 9×5-inch pans; loaves will be slightly shorter.*

Irish Soda Bread

makes 1 loaf

- **4 cups all-purpose flour**
- **¼ cup sugar**
- **4 teaspoons baking powder**
- **1 teaspoon salt**
- **½ teaspoon baking soda**
- **½ cup (1 stick) cold butter, cut into pieces**
- **1 cup currants**
- **2 teaspoons caraway seeds (optional)**
- **1⅓ cups buttermilk**

1 Preheat oven to 350°F. Line baking sheet with parchment paper or spray with nonstick cooking spray.

2 Whisk flour, sugar, baking powder, salt and baking soda in large bowl. Cut in butter with pastry blender or fingertips until mixture resembles coarse crumbs. Stir in currants and caraway seeds, if desired. Add buttermilk; mix until slightly sticky dough forms. Transfer dough to prepared baking sheet; shape into 8-inch round.

3 Bake 50 to 60 minutes or until bread is golden brown and crust is firm. Cool on baking sheet 10 minutes. Remove to wire rack; cool completely.

Tip: For a sweet crust, combine 1 tablespoon sugar and 1 tablespoon water in small bowl; brush over hot loaf.

Peanut Butter Chocolate Chip Bread

makes 1 loaf

- **1½ cups all-purpose flour**
- **2 teaspoons baking powder**
- **¼ teaspoon salt**
- **¼ teaspoon ground cinnamon**
- **¼ teaspoon ground nutmeg**
- **⅔ cup milk**
- **1 teaspoon vanilla**
- **¾ cup packed dark brown sugar**
- **½ cup vegetable oil**
- **½ cup creamy peanut butter**
- **2 eggs**
- **1 cup finely chopped roasted salted peanuts**
- **1 cup mini semisweet chocolate chips**

1. Preheat oven to 350°F. Spray 9×5-inch loaf pan with nonstick cooking spray or line with parchment paper.

2. Whisk flour, baking powder, salt, cinnamon and nutmeg in medium bowl. Combine milk and vanilla in small bowl.

3. Beat brown sugar, oil and peanut butter in large bowl until well blended. Add eggs, one at a time, beating until well blended after each addition. Add flour mixture alternately with milk mixture, beating at low speed just until blended. Stir in peanuts and chocolate chips. Spread batter in prepared pan.

4. Bake about 1 hour or until toothpick inserted into center comes out clean. Cool in pan 15 minutes. Remove to wire rack; cool completely.

Simple Golden Corn Bread

makes 9 to 12 servings

1¼ cups all-purpose flour
¾ cup yellow cornmeal
⅓ cup sugar
2 teaspoons baking powder
1 teaspoon salt
1¼ cups whole milk
¼ cup (½ stick) butter, melted
1 egg
Honey Butter (recipe follows, optional)

1 Preheat oven to 400°F. Spray 8-inch square baking pan with nonstick cooking spray.

2 Whisk flour, cornmeal, sugar, baking powder and salt in large bowl. Whisk milk, butter and egg in medium bowl until well blended. Add to flour mixture; stir just until dry ingredients are moistened. Pour batter into prepared pan.

3 Bake 25 minutes or until golden brown and toothpick inserted into center comes out clean. Prepare Honey Butter, if desired; serve with corn bread.

Honey Butter: Beat 6 tablespoons softened butter and ¼ cup honey in medium bowl with electric mixer at medium-high speed until light and creamy.

Glazed Lemon Loaf

makes 1 loaf

Bread

- **1½ cups all-purpose flour**
- **½ teaspoon baking powder**
- **½ teaspoon baking soda**
- **½ teaspoon salt**
- **1 cup granulated sugar**
- **3 eggs**
- **½ cup vegetable oil**
- **⅓ cup lemon juice**
- **2 tablespoons butter, melted**
- **1 teaspoon lemon extract**
- **½ teaspoon vanilla**

Glaze

- **3 tablespoons butter**
- **1½ cups powdered sugar**
- **2 tablespoons lemon juice**
- **1 to 2 teaspoons grated lemon peel**

1 Preheat oven to 350°F. Spray 8×4-inch loaf pan with nonstick cooking spray.

2 For bread, whisk flour, baking powder, baking soda and salt in large bowl. Whisk granulated sugar, eggs, oil, ⅓ cup lemon juice, 2 tablespoons melted butter, lemon extract and vanilla in medium bowl until well blended. Add to flour mixture; stir just until blended. Pour batter into prepared pan.

3 Bake about 40 minutes or until toothpick inserted into center comes out clean. Cool in pan 10 minutes. Remove to wire rack; cool 10 minutes.

4 Meanwhile for glaze, melt 3 tablespoons butter in small saucepan over medium-low heat. Whisk in powdered sugar, 2 tablespoons lemon juice and 1 teaspoon lemon peel; cook until smooth and hot, whisking constantly. Pour glaze over warm bread; smooth top. Cool completely before slicing. Garnish with additional 1 teaspoon lemon peel, if desired.

Gingerbread

makes 9 to 12 servings

- 2 cups all-purpose flour
- 2 teaspoons ground ginger
- ½ teaspoon baking powder
- ½ teaspoon baking soda
- ½ teaspoon salt
- ½ teaspoon ground cinnamon
- 1 cup ginger ale
- ¾ cup packed brown sugar
- 6 tablespoons butter, melted and cooled
- ½ cup molasses
- 2 eggs
- 1 tablespoon grated fresh ginger
- Whipped cream (optional)

1 Preheat oven to 350°F. Spray 9-inch square baking pan with nonstick cooking spray.

2 Whisk flour, ground ginger, baking powder, baking soda, salt and cinnamon in medium bowl. Whisk ginger ale, brown sugar, butter, molasses, eggs and grated ginger in large bowl until well blended. Add flour mixture in two additions, stirring until well blended after each addition. Pour batter into prepared pan.

3 Bake 30 to 35 minutes or until toothpick inserted into center comes out clean. Cool in pan 10 minutes. Remove to wire rack; cool slightly. Serve warm or at room temperature with whipped cream, if desired.

Fruit and Nut Loaf

makes 1 loaf

- **1½ cups all-purpose flour**
- **½ cup whole wheat flour**
- **¼ cup sugar**
- **1 tablespoon baking powder**
- **¾ teaspoon baking soda**
- **¼ teaspoon salt**
- **1 cup orange juice**
- **3 eggs**
- **¼ cup vegetable oil**
- **1 tablespoon grated orange peel**
- **½ teaspoon vanilla**
- **¾ cup mixed dried fruit**
- **¼ cup chopped pecans**

1 Preheat oven to 350°F. Spray 8×4-inch loaf pan with nonstick cooking spray.

2 Whisk all-purpose flour, whole wheat flour, sugar, baking powder, baking soda and salt in medium bowl.

3 Whisk orange juice, eggs, oil, orange peel and vanilla in large bowl until well blended. Gradually add flour mixture, stirring just until blended. Stir in fruit and pecans. Pour batter into prepared pan.

4 Bake 35 to 40 minutes or until toothpick inserted into center comes out clean. Cool in pan 10 minutes. Remove to wire rack; cool completely.

Rhubarb Bread

makes 1 loaf

- **2 cups all-purpose flour**
- **1 cup sugar**
- **1 tablespoon baking powder**
- **1 teaspoon salt**
- **¼ teaspoon ground cinnamon**
- **1 cup milk**
- **2 eggs**
- **½ cup (1 stick) butter, melted**
- **2 teaspoons grated fresh ginger or orange peel**
- **10 ounces chopped fresh rhubarb (¼-inch pieces, about 2¼ cups)**
- **¾ cup chopped walnuts, toasted***

To toast walnuts, cook in medium skillet over medium heat 3 to 4 minutes or until lightly browned and fragrant, stirring frequently.

1 Preheat oven to 350°F. Spray 9×5-inch loaf pan with nonstick cooking spray.

2 Whisk flour, sugar, baking powder, salt and cinnamon in large bowl. Whisk milk, eggs, butter and ginger in medium bowl until well blended. Add to flour mixture; stir just until dry ingredients are moistened. Add rhubarb and walnuts; stir just until blended. Pour batter into prepared pan.

3 Bake about 1 hour or until toothpick inserted into center comes out clean. Cool in pan 15 minutes. Remove to wire rack; cool completely.

Cheddar Quick Bread

makes 1 loaf

- 2 cups all-purpose flour
- 4 teaspoons baking powder
- 1 tablespoon sugar
- ½ teaspoon salt
- ½ teaspoon onion powder
- ½ to 1 teaspoon dry mustard
- 1½ cups (6 ounces) shredded Cheddar cheese
- 1 cup milk
- 1 egg
- 2 tablespoons butter, melted

1 Preheat oven to 350°F. Spray 8×4-inch loaf pan with nonstick cooking spray.

2 Whisk flour, baking powder, sugar, salt, onion powder and mustard in large bowl. Stir in cheese until well blended. Whisk milk, egg and butter in medium bowl until well blended. Add to flour mixture; stir just until combined. Spread batter in prepared pan.

3 Bake 40 to 45 minutes or until toothpick inserted into center comes out clean. Cool in pan 10 minutes. Remove to wire rack; serve warm or cool completely.

Loaded Banana Bread

makes 1 loaf

- **1½ cups all-purpose flour**
- **2½ teaspoons baking powder**
- **¼ teaspoon salt**
- **6 tablespoons butter, softened**
- **⅓ cup granulated sugar**
- **⅓ cup packed brown sugar**
- **2 eggs**
- **3 ripe bananas, mashed**
- **½ teaspoon vanilla**
- **1 can (8 ounces) crushed pineapple, drained**
- **⅓ cup flaked sweetened coconut**
- **¼ cup mini chocolate chips**
- **⅓ cup chopped walnuts (optional)**

1 Preheat oven to 350°F. Spray 9×5-inch loaf pan with nonstick cooking spray.

2 Whisk flour, baking powder and salt in small bowl. Beat butter, granulated sugar and brown sugar in large bowl with electric mixer at medium speed about 3 minutes or until light and fluffy. Add eggs, one at a time, beating until well blended after each addition. Add bananas and vanilla; beat just until blended.

3 Gradually add flour mixture at low speed, beating just until blended. Fold in pineapple, coconut and chocolate chips. Spread batter in prepared pan; top with walnuts, if desired.

4 Bake 50 minutes or until toothpick inserted into center comes out with a few moist crumbs. Cool in pan 1 hour. Remove to wire rack; cool completely.

Muffins, Scones & Biscuits

Rosemary Parmesan Biscuit Poppers

makes 2 dozen mini biscuits

2¼ cups biscuit baking mix
⅔ cup milk
⅓ cup grated Parmesan cheese, divided
1 tablespoon chopped fresh rosemary *or* 1 teaspoon dried rosemary, crushed
1 tablespoon grated lemon peel
⅛ teaspoon ground red pepper
3 tablespoons olive oil
Kosher salt or flaky salt

1 Preheat oven to 450°F. Line baking sheet with parchment paper or spray with nonstick cooking spray.

2 Combine biscuit mix, milk, ¼ cup cheese, rosemary, lemon peel and red pepper in medium bowl; mix well. Drop dough by teaspoonfuls in 1-inch mounds onto prepared baking sheet. Sprinkle with remaining cheese.

3 Bake 8 to 10 minutes or until golden brown. Brush biscuits with oil; sprinkle with salt, if desired. Serve immediately.

White Chocolate Chunk Muffins

makes 12 jumbo muffins

- **2½ cups all-purpose flour**
- **1 cup packed brown sugar**
- **⅓ cup unsweetened cocoa powder**
- **2 teaspoons baking soda**
- **½ teaspoon salt**
- **1⅓ cups buttermilk**
- **¼ cup (½ stick) plus 2 tablespoons butter, melted**
- **2 eggs**
- **1½ teaspoons vanilla**
- **1½ cups chopped white chocolate**

1 Preheat oven to 400°F. Line 12 jumbo (3½-inch) muffin cups with paper baking cups or spray with nonstick cooking spray.

2 Whisk flour, brown sugar, cocoa, baking soda and salt in large bowl. Whisk buttermilk, butter, eggs and vanilla in small bowl until blended. Stir into flour mixture just until moistened. Fold in white chocolate. Spoon batter evenly into prepared muffin cups, filling about half full.

3 Bake 25 to 30 minutes or until toothpick inserted into centers comes out clean. Cool in pan on wire rack 5 minutes. Remove to wire rack; serve warm or cool completely.

Oat and Whole Wheat Scones

makes 8 scones

- 1 cup old-fashioned oats
- 1 cup whole wheat flour
- ½ cup all-purpose flour
- ¼ cup sugar
- 1 tablespoon baking powder
- ¼ teaspoon salt
- ½ cup (1 stick) cold butter, cut into pieces
- ½ cup whipping cream
- 1 egg
- ¾ cup dried cherries

1 Preheat oven to 425°F. Line baking sheet with parchment paper.

2 Whisk oats, whole wheat flour, all-purpose flour, sugar, baking powder and salt in large bowl. Cut in butter with pastry blender or fingertips until mixture resembles coarse crumbs. Whisk cream and egg in small bowl. Add to flour mixture; stir just until dough comes together. Stir in cherries.

3 Turn out dough onto lightly floured surface. Shape dough into 8-inch disc about ¾ inch thick. Cut into eight wedges; place 1 inch apart on prepared baking sheet.

4 Bake 18 to 20 minutes or until golden brown. Remove to wire rack; serve warm.

Sun-Dried Tomato Basil Muffins

makes 12 muffins

- **½ cup sun-dried tomatoes (about 12 pieces, not oil-packed)**
- **2 cups all-purpose flour**
- **1 tablespoon baking powder**
- **1½ teaspoons dried basil**
- **½ teaspoon salt**
- **¼ teaspoon black pepper**
- **⅛ teaspoon garlic powder**
- **¾ cup milk**
- **½ cup cottage cheese**
- **1 egg**
- **3 tablespoons vegetable oil**
- **2 teaspoons minced dried onion**

1 Preheat oven to 400°F. Spray 12 standard (2½-inch) muffin cups with nonstick cooking spray or line with paper baking cups.

2 Cover sun-dried tomatoes with hot water in small bowl; let stand 10 minutes to soften. Drain and finely chop.

3 Whisk flour, baking powder, basil, salt, pepper and garlic powder in medium bowl. Whisk milk, cottage cheese, egg, oil, onion and tomatoes in large bowl until well blended. Add flour mixture; stir just until blended. Spoon batter evenly into prepared muffin cups.

4 Bake 20 to 25 minutes or until toothpick inserted into centers comes out clean. Cool in pan 5 minutes. Remove to wire rack; serve warm or cool completely.

Green Onion Biscuits

makes 8 biscuits

2 cups all-purpose flour
1 tablespoon baking powder
1 tablespoon sugar
¾ teaspoon salt
3 ounces cold cream cheese
¼ cup (½ stick) cold butter, cut into pieces
½ cup finely chopped green onions
⅔ cup milk

1 Preheat oven to 450°F.

2 Whisk flour, baking powder, sugar and salt in medium bowl. Cut in cream cheese and butter with pastry blender or fingertips until mixture resembles coarse crumbs. Stir in green onions.

3 Make well in center of flour mixture. Add milk; stir until mixture forms soft dough that clings together and forms a ball.

4 Turn out dough onto well-floured surface; knead gently 10 to 12 times. Roll or pat dough to ½-inch thickness. Cut out biscuits with floured 3-inch round cutter. Place biscuits 2 inches apart on ungreased baking sheet.

5 Bake 10 to 12 minutes or until golden brown. Remove to wire rack; serve warm.

Cheese Biscuits

makes 12 biscuits

- 2 cups all-purpose flour
- 2¼ teaspoons baking powder
- 1½ teaspoons sugar
- ¾ teaspoon salt
- ¼ teaspoon baking soda
- ½ cup (1 stick) cold butter, cut into pieces
- 1 cup (4 ounces) shredded Cheddar cheese
- ½ cup (2 ounces) shredded Gruyère or Swiss cheese
- 3 tablespoons grated Parmesan cheese
- 1 cup buttermilk
- 1 tablespoon butter, melted

1 Whisk flour, baking powder, sugar, salt and baking soda in large bowl. Cut in cold butter with pastry blender or fingertips until coarse crumbs form. Stir in Cheddar, Gruyère and Parmesan; toss to blend. Make a well in center of flour mixture; pour in buttermilk. Stir just until blended; do not overmix. Cover and refrigerate 20 minutes.

2 Preheat oven to 375°F. Line baking sheet with parchment paper. Scoop dough into 12 mounds onto prepared baking sheet.

3 Bake 13 to 15 minutes or until golden brown. Brush melted butter over tops of biscuits. Serve warm.

Blueberry Muffins

makes 12 muffins

- **2 cups all-purpose flour**
- **2¼ teaspoons baking powder**
- **½ teaspoon salt**
- **¼ teaspoon baking soda**
- **1 cup granulated sugar**
- **½ cup (1 stick) butter, melted**
- **¾ cup buttermilk**
- **2 eggs**
- **1 teaspoon grated lemon peel**
- **1½ cups blueberries**
- **2 tablespoons sparkling sugar *or* 4 tablespoons turbinado sugar**

1 Preheat oven to 375°F. Line 12 standard (2½-inch) muffin cups with paper baking cups or spray with nonstick cooking spray.

2 Whisk flour, baking powder, salt and baking soda in medium bowl. Whisk granulated sugar and butter in large bowl until well blended. Add buttermilk, eggs and lemon peel; whisk until well blended. Add flour; stir just until dry ingredients are moistened. Gently fold in blueberries.

3 Spoon batter into prepared muffin cups (cups will be almost full). Sprinkle ½ teaspoon sparkling sugar or 1 teaspoon turbinado sugar over each muffin.

4 Bake 20 to 22 minutes or until toothpick inserted into centers comes out clean. Cool in pan 5 minutes. Remove to wire rack; serve warm or cool completely.

Cranberry Chocolate Chunk Muffins

makes 12 muffins

- **1¾ cups all-purpose flour**
- **½ cup sugar**
- **1½ teaspoons baking powder**
- **½ teaspoon salt**
- **½ cup milk**
- **½ cup vegetable oil**
- **2 eggs**
- **1 teaspoon vanilla**
- **¾ cup coarsely chopped pecans, toasted***
- **¾ cup chopped semisweet chocolate**
- **½ cup dried cranberries**

****To toast pecans, cook in medium skillet over medium heat 3 to 4 minutes or until lightly browned and fragrant, stirring frequently.***

1 Preheat oven to 350°F. Line 12 standard (2½-inch) muffin cups with paper baking cups or spray with nonstick cooking spray.

2 Whisk flour, sugar, baking powder and salt in large bowl. Add milk, oil, eggs and vanilla; mix well. Add pecans, chocolate chunks and dried cranberries; mix well. Spoon batter evenly into prepared muffin cups.

3 Bake 15 minutes or until toothpick inserted into centers comes out clean. Cool in pan 5 minutes. Remove to wire rack; serve warm or cool completely.

Dark Chocolate Cherry Scones

makes 8 scones

- 2½ cups all-purpose flour
- ½ cup (1 stick) cold butter, cut into pieces
- 1 tablespoon baking powder
- 1 tablespoon plus 2 teaspoons sugar, divided
- ⅛ teaspoon salt
- 4 ounces dark chocolate, chopped (about 1 cup)
- ½ cup dried cherries
- ¾ cup plus 2 tablespoons whipping cream, divided
- 2 whole eggs
- 1 egg yolk
- 2 teaspoons sugar

1 Preheat oven to 400°F. Line large baking sheet with parchment paper.

2 Combine flour, butter, baking powder, 1 tablespoon sugar and salt in food processor or blender; pulse until mixture resembles coarse crumbs. Add chocolate and cherries; pulse three times.

3 With motor running, add ¾ cup cream and 2 whole eggs through feed tube; process until dough forms a ball. Transfer dough to lightly floured surface; divide in half. Pat into two 6-inch circles about ½ inch thick; cut each into quarters. Place 2 inches apart on prepared baking sheet. Whisk egg yolk and remaining 2 tablespoons cream in small bowl. Brush egg mixture over tops of scones; sprinkle with remaining 2 teaspoons sugar.

4 Bake 14 minutes or until golden brown. Remove to wire rack; cool slightly.

Chile Pecan Biscuits

makes about 10 biscuits

- ½ cup (1 stick) cold butter, divided
- 2 tablespoons minced jalapeño pepper
- ⅓ cup finely chopped pecans
- 1 tablespoon honey
- 2 cups all-purpose flour
- 1 tablespoon baking powder
- ½ teaspoon salt
- ⅛ teaspoon chipotle chili powder
- ¼ teaspoon ground cumin
- ¾ cup milk
- 5 tablespoons shredded sharp Cheddar cheese (optional)

1 Preheat oven to 425°F. Line baking sheet with parchment paper or spray with nonstick cooking spray.

2 Melt 1 tablespoon butter in small skillet over medium heat. Add jalapeño and pecans; cook and stir 3 to 5 minutes or until jalapeño is tender and pecans are fragrant. Stir in honey; set aside to cool.

3 Whisk flour, baking powder, salt, chili powder and cumin in large bowl. Cut remaining 7 tablespoons butter into pieces; add to flour mixture. Cut in butter with pastry blender or fingertips until mixture resembles coarse crumbs. Stir in pecan mixture and milk.

4 Turn out dough onto lightly floured surface; knead gently six to eight times. Pat to ¾-inch thickness. Cut out biscuits with 2½-inch biscuit cutter; gather and reroll scraps. Place 1 inch apart on prepared baking sheet. Pat about 1½ teaspoons cheese onto each biscuit, if desired.

5 Bake 15 to 17 minutes or until golden brown. Remove to wire rack; serve warm or cool completely.

Banana Chocolate Chip Muffins

makes 15 muffins

- 2 cups all-purpose flour
- ¼ cup granulated sugar
- ¼ cup packed brown sugar
- 1½ teaspoons baking powder
- ½ teaspoon salt
- ¼ teaspoon baking soda
- 1 cup mashed ripe bananas (about 2 large or 3 small)
- ½ cup (1 stick) butter, melted
- 2 eggs
- ⅓ cup buttermilk
- 1 teaspoon vanilla
- 1 package (12 ounces) semisweet chocolate chips

1 Preheat oven to 375°F. Spray 15 standard (2½-inch) muffin cups with nonstick cooking spray or line with paper baking cups.

2 Whisk flour, granulated sugar, brown sugar, baking powder, salt and baking soda in large bowl. Whisk bananas, butter, eggs, buttermilk and vanilla in medium bowl until well blended. Add to flour mixture; stir just until dry ingredients are moistened. Stir in chocolate chips. Spoon batter evenly into prepared muffin cups, filling almost full. Smooth tops.

3 Bake about 18 minutes or until toothpick inserted into centers comes out clean. Cool in pans 5 minutes. Remove to wire racks; serve warm or cool completely.

Note: If you want to use only one pan, you can divide the batter evenly among 12 standard muffin cups instead of 15 and fill the cups completely.

Banana Chocolate Chip Bread: Preheat oven to 350°F. Line 9×5-inch loaf pan with parchment paper; spray with nonstick cooking spray. Prepare batter as directed; spread in prepared pan. Bake about 1 hour 10 minutes or until toothpick inserted into center comes out clean. Cool in pan 10 minutes. Remove to wire rack; serve warm or cool completely.

Oat and Pecan Scones

makes 12 scones

- 1½ cups all-purpose flour
- ¾ cup old-fashioned oats, toasted*
- ½ cup raisins or currants
- ½ cup packed brown sugar
- 2½ teaspoons baking powder
- 1 teaspoon ground cinnamon
- ½ teaspoon baking soda
- ¼ teaspoon ground ginger
- ¼ teaspoon salt
- ½ cup (1 stick) cold butter, cut into pieces
- 1 cup chopped pecans, toasted**
- ⅔ to ¾ cup half-and-half or milk
- 2 teaspoons granulated sugar

***To toast oats, cook in large skillet over medium heat 1 to 2 minutes or until oats just begin to turn golden, stirring frequently. Immediately remove from skillet; cool before using.**

****To toast pecans, cook in medium skillet over medium heat 3 to 4 minutes or until lightly browned and fragrant, stirring frequently.**

1 Preheat oven to 425°F. Line baking sheet with parchment paper or spray with nonstick cooking spray.

2 Whisk flour, oats, raisins, brown sugar, baking powder, cinnamon, baking soda, ginger and salt in large bowl. Cut in butter with pastry blender or fingertips until mixture resembles coarse crumbs. Stir in pecans.

3 Gradually add half-and-half, stirring until dough comes together. Drop dough by ¼ cupfuls 1 inch apart onto prepared baking sheet. Sprinkle with granulated sugar.

4 Bake 15 to 17 minutes or until golden brown. Cool on baking sheet 5 minutes. Remove to wire rack; serve warm or at room temperature.

Yeast Breads

Upside-Down Apricot Pecan Rolls

makes 12 rolls

- **¼ cup pecan pieces**
- **2 tablespoons packed dark brown sugar**
- **2 teaspoons ground cinnamon**
- **1 package (11 ounces) refrigerated French bread dough**
- **5 tablespoons butter, softened, divided**
- **¼ cup granulated sugar**
- **¼ cup finely chopped dried apricots**

1 Preheat oven to 350°F. Spray 9-inch round nonstick baking pan with nonstick cooking spray. Sprinkle pecans, brown sugar and cinnamon evenly over bottom of pan.

2 Unroll dough on work surface. Spread 3 tablespoons butter evenly over dough. Sprinkle with granulated sugar. Top with apricots. Starting with long side, gently roll up dough jelly-roll style; pinch seam to seal. Cut log into 12 slices. Place slices cut sides up in prepared pan.

3 Bake 30 minutes or until golden brown. Immediately invert onto serving plate. Add remaining 2 tablespoons butter to hot pan; stir until melted. Drizzle over rolls.

Soft Beer Pretzels

makes 12 pretzels

- ¼ cup warm water
- 1 package (¼ ounce) active dry yeast
- 4 cups all-purpose flour
- 1 cup brown ale, at room temperature
- 1 tablespoon sugar
- 1 tablespoon olive oil
- 1 teaspoon kosher salt, divided
- 2 cups hot water
- 1 teaspoon baking soda
- 1 egg, well beaten
- 2 tablespoons butter, melted

1 Combine warm water and yeast in large bowl; stir until dissolved. Let stand 5 minutes or until mixture is bubbly. Add flour, ale, sugar, oil and ¾ teaspoon salt; stir to form soft dough. Turn out dough onto lightly floured surface. Knead 6 to 8 minutes or until smooth and elastic, adding additional flour by tablespoonfuls if necessary.*

2 Place dough in greased bowl; turn to grease top. Cover and let rise in warm place 45 minutes or until doubled in size.

3 Punch down dough. Divide into 12 pieces. Roll each piece into a rope about 20 inches long. If dough becomes too difficult to roll, let stand 10 minutes. Shape ropes into pretzels.

4 Preheat oven to 425°F. Line baking sheet with parchment paper or spray with nonstick cooking spray. Stir hot water into baking soda in medium bowl until blended. Dip pretzels into mixture; place on prepared baking sheet. Cover loosely and let stand in warm place 15 to 20 minutes. Brush pretzels with egg; sprinkle with remaining ¼ teaspoon salt.

5 Bake 10 minutes or until golden brown. Brush pretzels with melted butter.

**To knead dough, fold dough in half toward you and press dough away from you with heels of hands. Give dough a quarter turn and continue folding, pushing and turning.*

Variation: Sprinkle a small amount of shredded cheese over pretzels before baking—Parmesan, Asiago or Cheddar are good choices. Or add ½ cup (2 ounces) shredded Cheddar cheese to dough when you are almost finished kneading in step 1.

Cinnamon Raisin Bread

makes 1 loaf

- 1 cup milk
- 3 tablespoons butter
- 3 to 3½ cups all-purpose flour, divided
- ½ cup sugar, divided
- 1 package (¼ ounce) active dry yeast
- 1 teaspoon salt
- 1 whole egg
- 1 egg, separated
- 1 teaspoon vanilla
- ¾ cup raisins
- 1 tablespoon ground cinnamon
- 1 tablespoon butter, melted
- 1 tablespoon water

1 Combine milk and 3 tablespoons butter in small saucepan; heat over low heat to 115° to 120°F (butter does not need to melt completely).

2 Combine 1½ cups flour, ¼ cup sugar, yeast and salt in large bowl of stand mixer. Gradually add milk mixture at low speed; beat at medium speed 2 minutes. Add whole egg, egg yolk and vanilla; beat 2 minutes.

3 Add 1½ cups flour; knead with dough hook at low speed 5 minutes or until dough is smooth and elastic, adding enough remaining flour by tablespoonfuls if needed to clean side of bowl. Add raisins; mix well. Shape dough into a ball. Place dough in greased bowl; turn to grease top. Cover and let rise in warm place about 1 hour or until doubled in size.

4 Punch down dough; knead on lightly floured surface 1 minute. Cover and let rest 10 minutes. Spray 9×5-inch loaf pan with nonstick cooking spray. Combine remaining ¼ cup sugar and cinnamon in small bowl; reserve 1 teaspoon mixture for top of loaf, if desired.

5 Roll out dough into 20×9-inch rectangle with lightly floured rolling pin. Brush with 1 tablespoon melted butter; sprinkle with remaining cinnamon-sugar. Starting with short side, roll up dough jelly-roll style; pinch seam and ends to seal. Place loaf, seam side down, in prepared pan; cover and let rise in warm place about 30 minutes or until doubled in size.

6 Preheat oven to 375°F. Beat egg white and water in small bowl until blended. Brush over top of loaf; sprinkle with reserved cinnamon-sugar.

7 Bake 40 to 45 minutes or until bread sounds hollow when tapped (internal temperature of 190°F). Cover loosely with foil halfway through baking time if bread is browning too fast. Remove to wire rack; cool completely.

Garlic Knots

makes 20 knots

- 1 package (¼ ounce) active dry yeast
- 1 teaspoon sugar
- ¾ cup warm water (105° to 115°F)
- 2¼ cups all-purpose flour
- 2 tablespoons olive oil, divided
- 1½ teaspoons salt, divided
- 4 tablespoons (½ stick) butter, divided
- 1 tablespoon minced garlic
- ¼ teaspoon garlic powder
- ½ cup grated Parmesan cheese
- 2 tablespoons chopped fresh parsley
- ½ teaspoon dried oregano

1 Dissolve yeast and sugar in warm water in large bowl of stand mixer; let stand 5 minutes or until bubbly. Add flour, 1 tablespoon oil and 1 teaspoon salt; knead with dough hook at low speed 5 minutes or until dough is smooth and elastic.

2 Shape dough into a ball. Place dough in greased bowl; turn to grease top. Cover and let rise in warm place 1 hour or until doubled in size.

3 Melt 2 tablespoons butter in small saucepan over low heat. Add remaining 1 tablespoon oil, ½ teaspoon salt, minced garlic and garlic powder; cook over very low heat 5 minutes. Pour into small bowl; set aside.

4 Preheat oven to 400°F. Line baking sheet with parchment paper.

5 Punch down dough. Turn out dough onto lightly floured surface; let rest 10 minutes. Roll out dough into 10×8-inch rectangle; cut into 20 (2-inch) squares. Roll each piece into 8-inch rope; tie in a knot. Place knots on prepared baking sheet; brush with butter mixture.

6 Bake 10 minutes or until lightly browned. Meanwhile, melt remaining 2 tablespoons butter. Combine cheese, parsley and oregano in small bowl; mix well. Brush melted butter over knots immediately after baking; sprinkle with cheese mixture. Cool slightly; serve warm.

Brown Bread

makes 2 loaves

- **1 package (¼ ounce) active dry yeast**
- **1¼ cups warm water (105° to 110°F)**
- **¼ cup packed brown sugar**
- **¼ cup molasses**
- **2 tablespoons vegetable oil**
- **1½ tablespoons unsweetened cocoa powder**
- **1¼ teaspoons salt**
- **2 cups all-purpose flour**
- **1½ cups whole wheat flour**
- **2 teaspoons old-fashioned oats**

1 Dissolve yeast in warm water in large bowl of stand mixer; let stand 5 minutes or until bubbly. Stir in brown sugar, molasses, oil, cocoa and salt until well blended. Add all-purpose flour and whole wheat flour; stir until rough dough forms.

2 Knead with dough hook at low speed 5 minutes (dough will be slightly sticky but should clean side of bowl). Shape dough into a ball. Place dough in greased bowl; turn to grease top. Cover and let rise in warm place 1½ to 2 hours or until doubled in size.

3 Line baking sheet with parchment paper. Turn out dough onto very lightly floured surface; divide in half. Shape each half into 12×3-inch loaf; place loaves on prepared baking sheet. Moisten top and sides of loaves with dampened hands; sprinkle 1 teaspoon oats over top and sides of each loaf, pressing lightly to adhere. Loosely cover loaves and let rise in warm place 1 hour or until very puffy and almost doubled in height.

4 Preheat oven to 350°F. Bake 25 minutes or until bottoms of loaves are lightly browned (internal temperature is 190°F). Remove to wire racks; cool 10 minutes. Serve warm or cool completely.

Gannat (French Cheese Bread)

makes 1 loaf

- 1 package (¼ ounce) active dry yeast
- 1 teaspoon sugar
- 4 to 6 tablespoons warm water (105° to 115°F)
- 2½ cups all-purpose flour
- ¼ cup (½ stick) butter, softened
- 1 teaspoon salt
- 2 eggs
- 1 cup (4 ounces) Emmentaler Swiss, Gruyère, sharp Cheddar or Swiss cheese, shredded
- 1 teaspoon vegetable oil

1 Dissolve yeast and sugar in 4 tablespoons warm water in small bowl; let stand 5 minutes or until bubbly.

2 Combine flour, butter and salt in food processor; process 15 seconds or until blended. Add yeast mixture and eggs; process 15 seconds or just until blended.

3 With motor running, slowly drizzle in just enough water through feed tube until dough forms a ball that cleans side of bowl. Process until ball turns around bowl about 25 times. Let dough rest 1 to 2 minutes. With motor running, drizzle in enough remaining water to make dough soft, smooth and satiny. Process until dough turns around bowl about 15 times.

4 Turn out dough onto lightly floured surface; shape into a ball. Place dough in greased bowl; turn to grease top. Cover and let rise in warm place about 1 hour or until doubled in size.

5 Spray 9-inch round cake pan with nonstick cooking spray. Punch down dough. Place dough on lightly greased surface; knead cheese into dough. Roll or pat into 8-inch circle; brush with oil. Place in prepared pan. Cover and let rise in warm place about 45 minutes or until doubled in size. Preheat oven to 375°F.

6 Bake 30 to 35 minutes or until top is browned and bread sounds hollow when tapped. Remove to wire rack; cool completely.

Quattro Formaggio Focaccia

makes 12 servings

- 1¼ cups warm water (100° to 105°F)
- 1 tablespoon sugar
- 1 package (¼ ounce) active dry or instant yeast
- 3 to 3¼ cups all-purpose flour
- ¼ cup plus 2 tablespoons olive oil, divided
- 1 teaspoon salt
- ¼ cup marinara sauce with basil
- 1 cup (4 ounces) shredded Italian cheese blend

1 Combine warm water, sugar and yeast in large bowl of stand mixer; stir until dissolved. Let stand 5 minutes or until bubbly. Stir in 3 cups flour, ¼ cup oil and salt with spoon to form rough dough. Knead with dough hook at low speed 5 minutes, adding additional flour, 1 tablespoon at a time, if necessary for dough to come together. (Dough will be sticky and will not clean side of bowl.)

2 Scoop dough into greased bowl (dough may be too soft to shape into a ball); turn to grease top. Cover and let rise in warm place 1 to 1½ hours or until doubled in size.

3 Pour remaining 2 tablespoons oil into 13×9-inch baking pan. Turn out dough into pan; pat and stretch dough to fill pan. Dimple dough all over with fingertips.

4 Spread marinara sauce evenly over dough; sprinkle with cheese. Cover and let rise in warm place 30 minutes or until puffy. Preheat oven to 425°F.

5 Bake 17 to 20 minutes or until golden brown. Cool in pan 10 minutes. Remove to cutting board; cut into squares or strips.

Chocolate Buns

makes 8 rolls

- 1 cup plus 1 tablespoon milk, divided
- 3 tablespoons butter
- 3 to 3½ cups all-purpose flour
- 3 tablespoons granulated sugar
- 1 package (¼ ounce) active dry or instant yeast
- 1 teaspoon salt
- 1 egg
- 1 chocolate bar (6 ounces), cut into 16 pieces
- 2 teaspoons colored sugar

1 Combine 1 cup milk and butter in small saucepan. Heat over low heat until mixture is 120° to 130°F. (Butter does not need to completely melt.) Combine 3 cups flour, granulated sugar, yeast and salt in large bowl of stand mixture. Add milk mixture and egg; beat at medium speed until blended. Knead with dough hook at low speed 5 to 7 minutes or until dough is smooth and elastic, adding additional flour if needed to clean side of bowl.

2 Shape dough into a ball. Place in greased bowl; turn to grease top. Cover and let rise in warm place about 1 hour or until doubled in size.

3 Turn out dough onto lightly floured surface; knead 1 minute. Roll and shape into loaf. Cut loaf into eight pieces. Roll one dough piece into 6-inch round. Place two pieces of chocolate in center. Fold edges into center around chocolate; pinch and roll across surface to seal. Place seam side down on lightly greased baking sheet. Repeat with remaining dough pieces, arranging rolls 3 inches apart.

4 Cover and let rise in warm place 20 to 30 minutes or until slightly puffed. Brush tops with remaining 1 tablespoon milk. Sprinkle with colored sugar.

5 Preheat oven to 400°F. Bake 12 to 15 minutes or until rolls are golden brown. Remove to wire rack; serve warm.

Twisted Tomato Cheese Bread

makes 1 loaf

- **1 loaf (1 pound) frozen bread dough, thawed according to package directions**
- **⅓ cup plus 2 tablespoons pizza sauce, divided**
- **1 cup (4 ounces) shredded mozzarella cheese**
- **½ cup shredded Parmesan cheese**
- **1 egg, beaten**

1 Preheat oven to 350°F. Line 9×5-inch loaf pan with parchment paper or spray with nonstick cooking spray.

2 Roll out dough into 20×10-inch rectangle on lightly floured surface. Spread ⅓ cup pizza sauce evenly over dough, leaving ½-inch borders. Sprinkle with mozzarella and Parmesan. Starting with long side, roll up dough jelly-roll style; pinch seam to seal. Cut roll in half lengthwise; turn halves cut sides up. Twist halves together, keeping filling facing up as much as possible.

3 Arrange dough in prepared pan, winding twisted dough back and forth in pan. Brush top of dough with egg. Fill in crevices and folds of dough with spoonfuls of remaining pizza sauce.

4 Bake about 40 minutes or until bread is golden brown and cooked through. (Cover loosely with foil if dough browns too quickly.) Cool in pan on wire rack 10 minutes. Serve warm.

Pretzel Monkey Bread

makes 12 servings

- **2½ cups all-purpose flour**
- **1½ teaspoons instant or active dry yeast**
- **1 teaspoon sugar**
- **¼ teaspoon salt**
- **¾ cup warm water (120°F)**
- **6 tablespoons butter, melted, divided**
- **12 cups water**
- **½ cup baking soda**
- **Coarse salt**

Dipping Sauce

- **6 tablespoons sour cream**
- **2 tablespoons Dijon mustard**
- **1 tablespoon honey**

1 Combine flour, yeast, sugar and ¼ teaspoon salt in large bowl of stand mixer. Stir in ¾ cup water and 2 tablespoons melted butter to form rough dough. Knead with dough hook at low speed 5 to 7 minutes or until dough is smooth and elastic. Shape dough into a ball. Place in greased bowl; turn to grease top. Cover and let rise in warm place about 1 hour or until doubled in size.

2 Preheat oven to 400°F. Line baking sheet with foil. Brush 9-inch springform pan with 1 tablespoon butter; place on prepared baking sheet. Spray outside of 6-ounce ramekin with nonstick cooking spray; place in center of pan. Turn out dough onto lightly floured surface; pat and stretch into 12×6-inch rectangle. Cut dough into 1-inch pieces.

3 Bring 12 cups water to a boil in large saucepan; add baking soda. Working in batches, add dough pieces to boiling water; cook 30 seconds. Place half of boiled dough pieces around ramekin in prepared pan; brush with half of remaining butter and sprinkle with coarse salt. Top with remaining dough pieces; brush with remaining butter and sprinkle with coarse salt.

4 Bake about 30 minutes or until tops of pretzels are dark golden brown. Loosen edges of bread with knife; carefully remove side of pan.

5 For dipping sauce, combine sour cream, mustard and honey in small bowl. Carefully remove hot ramekin from center of pretzel ring and replace with bowl of sauce. (Ramekin from oven will be too hot for sauce.) Serve warm.

Honey-Pecan Coffeecake

makes 12 servings

- ⅔ cup milk
- 6 tablespoons butter, softened
- 9 tablespoons honey, divided
- 3½ cups all-purpose flour, divided
- 1 package (¼ ounce) active dry or instant yeast
- ¾ teaspoon salt
- 3 eggs, divided
- 1¼ cups toasted* coarsely chopped pecans, divided
- 3 tablespoons brown sugar
- 1½ tablespoons butter, melted
- 1 tablespoon ground cinnamon
- 1 teaspoon water

**To toast pecans, cook in medium skillet over medium heat 3 to 4 minutes or until lightly browned and fragrant, stirring frequently.*

1 Heat milk, softened butter and 3 tablespoons honey in small saucepan over low heat until temperature reaches 120° to 130°F. Combine 2½ cups flour, yeast and salt in large bowl of stand mixer. Add milk mixture and 2 eggs; beat at medium speed 2 minutes or until well blended. Gradually add additional flour until soft but rough dough forms. Knead with dough hook at low speed 5 to 7 minutes or until smooth and elastic, adding additional flour if needed to clean side of bowl.

2 Shape dough into ball. Place in greased bowl; turn to grease top. Let rise in warm place 40 minutes or until dough has increased in size by one third. Turn out onto lightly floured surface. Roll out into 14×8-inch rectangle using lightly floured rolling pin.

3 Combine 1 cup pecans, sugar, melted butter, cinnamon and 3 tablespoons honey in small bowl. Spread evenly over dough; press in gently with fingertips. Starting from one long end, roll up tightly, jelly-roll style. Pinch seams to seal; turn seam side down. Flatten slightly and twist dough 6 to 8 turns. Grease 9-inch round cake pan; place on baking sheet. Place dough in pan in loose spiral starting in center and working to the side. Tuck end under dough; pinch to seal. Loosely cover with lightly greased sheet of plastic wrap. Let rise in warm place about 1 hour or until doubled in size.

4 Preheat oven to 350°F. Beat remaining egg with 1 teaspoon water in small bowl; brush all over dough. Drizzle remaining 3 tablespoons honey evenly over top; sprinkle with remaining ¼ cup pecans.

5 Bake about 45 minutes or until deep golden brown. Turn pan and tent with sheet of foil halfway through baking time to prevent burning. Remove foil for last 5 minutes of baking. Cool in pan on wire rack 5 minutes. Remove to wire rack; cool completely.

Sweet & Savory Snacks

Mediterranean Flatbread

makes 16 pieces

- 2 tablespoons olive oil, divided
- ½ cup thinly sliced onion
- ½ cup thinly sliced red bell pepper
- ½ cup thinly sliced green bell pepper
- Salt and black pepper
- 1 package (11 ounces) refrigerated French bread dough
- 2 cloves garlic, minced
- ½ teaspoon dried rosemary
- ⅛ teaspoon red pepper flakes (optional)
- ⅓ cup pitted Kalamata olives, coarsely chopped
- ¼ cup grated Parmesan cheese

1 Preheat oven to 350°F. Line baking sheet with parchment paper or spray with nonstick cooking spray.

2 Heat 1 tablespoon oil in large skillet over medium-high heat. Add onion and bell peppers; cook and stir 5 minutes or until onion begins to brown. Remove from heat; season to taste with salt and black pepper.

3 Unroll dough on prepared baking sheet. Combine garlic and remaining 1 tablespoon oil in small bowl; spread evenly over dough. Sprinkle with rosemary and red pepper flakes, if desired. Top with onion mixture; sprinkle with olives.

4 Bake 16 to 18 minutes or until golden brown. Sprinkle with cheese. Cool on wire rack. Cut flatbread in half lengthwise; cut crosswise into 1-inch-wide strips.

Cookie Dough Monkey Bread

makes about 16 servings

- 1 package (about 16 ounces) break-apart refrigerated chocolate chip cookie dough (24 cookies)
- 2 packages (7½ ounces each) refrigerated buttermilk biscuits (10 biscuits per package)
- 1 cup semisweet chocolate chips, divided
- ¼ cup whipping cream

1 Preheat oven to 350°F. Generously spray 12-cup (10-inch) bundt pan with nonstick cooking spray.

2 Break cookie dough into 24 pieces; split each piece in half to create total of 48 pieces. Separate biscuits; cut each biscuit into four pieces with scissors. Layer half of cookie dough and half of biscuit pieces in prepared pan, alternating doughs. Sprinkle with ¼ cup chocolate chips. Repeat layers with remaining cookie dough and biscuit pieces; sprinkle with ¼ cup chocolate chips.

3 Bake 27 to 30 minutes or until biscuits are golden brown, covering pan loosely with foil during last 10 minutes of baking. Remove pan to wire rack; let stand, covered, 5 minutes. Loosen edges of bread with knife; invert onto serving plate.

4 Pour cream into medium microwavable bowl; microwave on HIGH 1 minute or until simmering. Add remaining ½ cup chocolate chips; stir until chocolate is melted. Let stand 5 minutes to thicken slightly. Drizzle glaze over bread.

Herb Cheese Twists

makes 10 twists

2 tablespoons butter
¼ cup grated Parmesan cheese
1 teaspoon dried parsley flakes
1 teaspoon dried basil
1 package (about 6 ounces) refrigerated buttermilk biscuits (5 biscuits)

1 Preheat oven to 400°F. Line baking sheet with parchment paper or spray with nonstick cooking spray.

2 Place butter in small microwavable bowl; microwave on MEDIUM (50%) 1 minute or just until melted. Cool slightly; stir in cheese, parsley flakes and basil.

3 Separate biscuits; stretch each biscuit into 5×2-inch rectangle. Spread 1 teaspoon butter mixture on each rectangle. Cut in half lengthwise; twist three or four times. Place on prepared baking sheet.

4 Bake 8 to 10 minutes or until golden brown.

Mocha Monkey Bread

makes 12 servings

Dough

- 1 cup warm water (120°F)
- 1 package (¼ ounce) active dry or instant yeast
- 3 cups all-purpose flour
- 3 tablespoons granulated sugar
- 2 tablespoons butter, melted
- 1 tablespoon unsweetened cocoa powder
- 1½ teaspoons salt
- 1 teaspoon instant espresso powder

Filling

- 5 tablespoons butter, melted, divided
- ¼ cup granulated sugar
- 1 tablespoon unsweetened cocoa powder
- 1 teaspoon instant espresso powder
- ¼ cup mini chocolate chips

Glaze

- 1 cup powdered sugar
- 1 teaspoon instant espresso powder
- 1 to 2 tablespoons half-and-half
- 2 tablespoons mini chocolate chips

1 For dough, combine water and yeast in large bowl of stand mixer; stir until dissolved. Let stand 5 minutes until bubbly. Add flour, 3 tablespoons granulated sugar, 2 tablespoons melted butter, 1 tablespoon cocoa, salt and 1 teaspoon espresso powder; stir to form rough dough. Knead with dough hook at low speed 5 to 7 minutes or until dough is smooth and elastic. Shape dough into a ball. Place in greased bowl; turn to grease top. Cover and let rise in warm place 30 to 45 minutes or until doubled in size.

2 Brush 12-cup (10-inch) bundt pan with 1 tablespoon melted butter. For filling, place remaining 4 tablespoons butter in medium bowl. Combine ¼ cup granulated sugar, 1 tablespoon cocoa and 1 teaspoon espresso powder in small bowl. Turn out dough onto lightly floured surface; pat into 12×6-inch rectangle. Cut dough into 1-inch squares; shape into balls. Dip balls in butter; roll in sugar mixture to coat. Layer half of balls in prepared

pan; sprinkle with ¼ cup chips. Top with remaining balls of dough. Cover and let rise in warm place about 30 minutes. Preheat oven to 350°F.

3 Bake about 25 minutes or until bread is firm and lightly browned. Immediately invert onto serving plate; cool slightly.

4 Meanwhile for glaze, combine powdered sugar and 1 teaspoon espresso powder in medium bowl. Stir in enough half-and-half to make thick, pourable glaze. Drizzle over bread; sprinkle with 2 tablespoons mini chips.

Olive Herb Pull-Aparts

makes 10 servings

- **2½ tablespoons olive oil, divided**
- **4 cloves garlic, minced**
- **1 package (12 ounces) refrigerated buttermilk biscuits (10 biscuits)**
- **¼ teaspoon red pepper flakes**
- **1 red onion, very thinly sliced**
- **½ cup shredded or chopped fresh basil**
- **½ (2¼-ounce) can sliced black olives, drained**
- **2 teaspoons chopped fresh rosemary**
- **¼ cup (1 ounce) crumbled feta cheese**

1 Preheat oven to 400°F. Line baking sheet with parchment paper or spray with nonstick cooking spray.

2 Combine 1½ tablespoons oil and garlic in small bowl. Separate biscuits; arrange on prepared baking sheet about ½ inch apart. Flatten biscuits. Sprinkle with red pepper flakes, gently pressing into biscuits. Brush with garlic oil; top with onion.

3 Combine basil, olives, rosemary and remaining 1 tablespoon oil in small bowl. Spread mixture over biscuits; sprinkle with cheese.

4 Bake 10 minutes or until golden brown. Serve warm or at room temperature.

Peanut Butter and Jelly Monkey Biscuits

makes 12 servings

¼ cup creamy peanut butter
2 tablespoons butter
2¼ cups all-purpose flour
¼ cup sugar
1 tablespoon baking powder
½ teaspoon salt
¼ cup (½ stick) cold butter, cut into small pieces
¾ cup buttermilk
6 tablespoons seedless strawberry jam, or favorite flavor

1 Preheat oven to 350°F. Line 9×5-inch loaf pan with foil, leaving 2-inch overhang. Spray foil with nonstick cooking spray.

2 Combine peanut butter and 2 tablespoons butter in small saucepan; cook and stir over low heat until melted. Cool slightly.

3 Whisk flour, sugar, baking powder and salt in medium bowl. Cut in ¼ cup cold butter with pastry blender or fingertips until mixture resembles coarse crumbs. Stir in buttermilk just until moistened.

4 Turn out dough onto lightly floured surface; knead six to eight times. Pat dough into 8×6-inch rectangle; cut into 1-inch squares. Roll one third of squares in peanut butter mixture to coat; place in single layer in prepared pan. Top with 2 tablespoons jam, dropping jam by spoonfuls evenly over squares. Repeat layers twice.

5 Bake 35 to 40 minutes or until jam is melted and bubbly and biscuits are flaky. Cool in pan on wire rack 10 minutes. Remove biscuits from pan using foil. Serve warm.

Spinach and Feta Stuffed Cheesy Bread

makes about 8 servings

- **1½ cups (6 ounces) shredded mozzarella or Monterey Jack cheese, divided**
- **1 cup (4 ounces) crumbled feta cheese**
- **¼ cup plus 1 tablespoon grated Parmesan cheese, divided**
- **1 teaspoon minced garlic**
- **1 container (11 ounces) refrigerated French bread dough**
- **1 cup baby spinach**
- **½ cup (2 ounces) shredded Cheddar cheese**
- **¼ teaspoon Italian seasoning or dried parsley flakes**

1 Preheat oven to 350°F. Line baking sheet with parchment paper.

2 Combine 1 cup mozzarella, feta, ¼ cup Parmesan and garlic in small bowl; mix well. Unroll dough on prepared baking sheet with long side facing you. Spread half of cheese mixture lengthwise over half of dough; top with spinach and remaining half of cheese mixture. Fold dough in half over filling; press long edge gently to seal.

3 Cut crosswise into 1-inch slices (but do not separate slices). Top with Cheddar, then with remaining ½ cup mozzarella. Sprinkle with Italian seasoning.

4 Bake 25 to 30 minutes or until golden brown. Serve warm.

Rosemary Wine Crackers

makes about 2 dozen crackers

1 cup whole wheat flour
1 tablespoon chopped fresh rosemary leaves
⅛ teaspoon salt
3 tablespoons olive oil
¼ cup wine (preferably a fruity white or rosé)
Coarse salt (optional)

1 Preheat oven to 400°F. Line baking sheet with parchment paper; dust lightly with flour.

2 Combine flour, rosemary and salt in food processor; pulse 30 seconds or until combined. With motor running, slowly add olive oil and wine until dough forms. Transfer to prepared baking sheet.

3 Roll out dough to ⅛-inch thickness. Sprinkle with coarse salt, if desired, pressing lightly into dough. Using tip of knife or pizza cutter, score dough into squares or diamonds.

4 Bake 10 to 15 minutes or until crackers begin to brown around edges, rotating baking sheet halfway through baking time. Remove to wire rack; cool completely. Break into individual crackers. Store in airtight container.

Tip: To re-crisp, place crackers in preheated 350°F oven and bake 5 minutes.

Bacon Cheddar Monkey Bread

makes 12 servings

- 1¾ cups (7 ounces) shredded sharp Cheddar cheese
- 12 ounces bacon, crisp-cooked and chopped (about 1 cup)
- ¼ cup finely chopped green onions
- 2¾ to 3 cups all-purpose flour, divided
- 1 package (¼ ounce) active dry or instant yeast
- 1 teaspoon salt
- 1 cup warm water (120°F)
- 2 tablespoons olive oil
- ⅓ cup butter, melted
- 1 egg

1 Combine cheese, bacon and green onions in medium bowl; mix well.

2 Combine 1½ cups flour, yeast and salt in large bowl of stand mixer. Add warm water and oil; beat at medium speed 3 minutes.

3 Knead with dough hook at low speed until dough comes together. Add 1 cup cheese mixture; knead 6 to 8 minutes or until dough is smooth and elastic, adding remaining ¼ cup flour if necessary to clean side of bowl. Shape dough into a ball. Place dough in greased bowl; turn to grease top. Cover and let rise in warm place 30 minutes or until doubled in size.

4 Generously spray 12-cup (10-inch) bundt pan with nonstick cooking spray. Beat butter and egg in shallow bowl until blended.

5 Punch down dough. Roll 1-inch pieces of dough into balls. Dip balls in butter mixture; roll in remaining cheese mixture to coat. Layer balls in prepared pan. Cover and let rise in warm place 30 minutes or until nearly doubled in size. Preheat oven to 375°F.

6 Bake 35 minutes or until golden brown. Loosen edges of bread with knife; invert onto serving plate. Cool 5 minutes; serve warm.

Cheddar Crisps

makes 32 crisps

- **1¾ cups all-purpose flour**
- **½ cup yellow cornmeal**
- **¾ teaspoon sugar**
- **¾ teaspoon salt**
- **½ teaspoon baking soda**
- **½ cup (1 stick) cold butter, cut into pieces**
- **1½ cups (6 ounces) shredded sharp Cheddar cheese**
- **½ cup cold water**
- **2 tablespoons white vinegar**
- **Coarsely ground black pepper**

1. Whisk flour, cornmeal, sugar, salt and baking soda in large bowl. Cut in butter with pastry blender or fingertips until mixture resembles coarse crumbs. Stir in cheese, water and vinegar with fork until mixture forms soft dough. Cover dough and refrigerate 1 hour or freeze 30 minutes or until firm.*

2. Preheat oven to 375°F. Spray two baking sheets with nonstick cooking spray or line with parchment paper. Divide dough into four pieces. Roll each piece into very thin circle, about 13 inches in diameter, on floured surface. Sprinkle with pepper; press pepper firmly into dough. Cut each circle into eight wedges; place on prepared baking sheets.

3. Bake about 10 minutes or until crisp. Store in airtight container up to 3 days.

**To prepare frozen dough, thaw in the refrigerator before proceeding with recipe as directed.*

Index

D

Metric Conversion Chart

VOLUME MEASUREMENTS (dry)

1/8 teaspoon = 0.5 mL
1/4 teaspoon = 1 mL
1/2 teaspoon = 2 mL
3/4 teaspoon = 4 mL
1 teaspoon = 5 mL
1 tablespoon = 15 mL
2 tablespoons = 30 mL
1/4 cup = 60 mL
1/3 cup = 75 mL
1/2 cup = 125 mL
2/3 cup = 150 mL
3/4 cup = 175 mL
1 cup = 250 mL
2 cups = 1 pint = 500 mL
3 cups = 750 mL
4 cups = 1 quart = 1 L

VOLUME MEASUREMENTS (fluid)

1 fluid ounce (2 tablespoons) = 30 mL
4 fluid ounces (1/2 cup) = 125 mL
8 fluid ounces (1 cup) = 250 mL
12 fluid ounces (1 1/2 cups) = 375 mL
16 fluid ounces (2 cups) = 500 mL

WEIGHTS (mass)

1/2 ounce = 15 g
1 ounce = 30 g
3 ounces = 90 g
4 ounces = 120 g
8 ounces = 225 g
10 ounces = 285 g
12 ounces = 360 g
16 ounces = 1 pound = 450 g

DIMENSIONS

1/16 inch = 2 mm
1/8 inch = 3 mm
1/4 inch = 6 mm
1/2 inch = 1.5 cm
3/4 inch = 2 cm
1 inch = 2.5 cm

OVEN TEMPERATURES

250°F = 120°C
275°F = 140°C
300°F = 150°C
325°F = 160°C
350°F = 180°C
375°F = 190°C
400°F = 200°C
425°F = 220°C
450°F = 230°C

BAKING PAN SIZES

Utensil	Size in Inches/Quarts	Metric Volume	Size in Centimeters
Baking or Cake Pan (square or rectangular)	8×8×2	2 L	20×20×5
	9×9×2	2.5 L	23×23×5
	12×8×2	3 L	30×20×5
	13×9×2	3.5 L	33×23×5
Loaf Pan	8×4×3	1.5 L	20×10×7
	9×5×3	2 L	23×13×7
Round Layer Cake Pan	8×1½	1.2 L	20×4
	9×1½	1.5 L	23×4
Pie Plate	8×1¼	750 mL	20×3
	9×1¼	1 L	23×3
Baking Dish or Casserole	1 quart	1 L	—
	1½ quart	1.5 L	—
	2 quart	2 L	—